Praise for *Eig*

"This new book by Rick Bliese is astoundingly original, accessible, and important for Christians seeking to bridge the gap between faith nurtured in church and their everyday lives in the real world. Themes familiar to those touched by 'faith at work' and 'ministry in daily life' movements come alive in fresh and radical ways through Bliese's creative use of the ancient image of the eighth day of creation: Monday, when resurrection life begins in Christ's new creation. Luther's Catechism becomes an unexpectedly empowering resource for disciples negotiating today's economic realities."

Phyllis Anderson, president emeritus,
Pacific Lutheran Theological Seminary

"In a world that is searching for social, racial, and economic justice and a church being challenged about its essence and core values, *Eighth-Day Discipleship* brings a fresh perspective about the way we connect our faith, work, and economics to our daily lives and our communities. It is an invitation for the restoration of God's creation through our humble obedience to God as coworkers with God. This means caring for the marginalized, the poor, the excluded, and those who differ from us. This book speaks the truth of the gospel to love, include, and celebrate strangers as equals and worthy of God's love."

Khader El-Yateem, assistant to the bishop and director for
evangelical mission, Florida-Bahamas Synod, ELCA

"Richard Bliese recaptures the vital Reformation shift, which we have neglected, from discipleship as laboring *for* victory, to grace-oriented, resurrection-powered discipleship working *from* victory—out in the real world of markets, family, neighborhood, and vocation. This book breathes a gust of Spirit-filled fresh air into this divided and contentious season of ecclesial defeatism, calling us away from our polarized silos and back to the Great Commission's central command to expand God's reign through disciple-making. And everyone gets to play; no one is left sitting on the bench."

David P. Householder, senior pastor at The Well at Surf City

"This book is deeply timely right now, for at least three reasons: First, Rick Bliese takes as his jumping-off point ordinary Christians' experiences of an economy marked these days by human fallenness, but also marked by human creativity, wisdom, and fruitful work. Second, he sees clearly and communicates winsomely that oft overlooked and misunderstood intersection between our economic and spiritual lives, namely the biblical concept of vocation. And third, against roiling and rising seas of cultural accommodation and political polarization, he brings us back to steady and faithful currents of Lutheran, Protestant, and, as C. S. Lewis once put it, 'mere Christian' tradition and catechism. This book helps us work out our salvation in both the world's economy and God's economy, for it is God who works in us."

Chris Armstrong, senior editor, *Christian History* magazine

"Rick Bliese has been the one pastor during the thirty years I've written and spoken on this subject who has understood why Martin Luther constructed a moral framework for primitive capitalism. Martin now hands his hammer to Rick to do the same for modern capitalism. Read this book."

Gary Moore, founder of The Financial Seminary

"Martin Luther's notion that 'vocation' is a gift to all Christians, rather than being the exclusive province of religious office, was a bombshell in the sixteenth century. It gave a dignity to ordinary life that was new, fresh, and bold. But in our own cultural context, 'vocation' has largely deteriorated into a commonplace synonym for 'how one earns a living.' Rick Bliese has shown us a way to recover the original power and significance of Luther's idea of vocation by reconnecting our work in the world with the essential structures of our faith, inviting us all to participate in the larger economy with renewed purpose, energy, commitment, and joy. This book is essential reading for anyone exploring the deep connections between faith and daily life."

Wayne N. Miller, bishop emeritus, Metropolitan Chicago Synod, ELCA

EIGHTH-DAY DISCIPLESHIP

EIGHTH-DAY
DISCIPLESHIP

A NEW VISION FOR
Faith, Work, and Economics

Richard H. Bliese

Foreword by John Arthur Nunes

FORTRESS PRESS
MINNEAPOLIS

I dedicate this book to Nina,
my wife of forty-three years.
The love of my life from day one.

Contents

Foreword   ix

Acknowledgments   xiii

Introduction:
An Evangelical Architecture for Eighth-Day Discipleship   1

1 Building Discipleship to Withstand Economic Storms   9

2 Connecting Faith and Work   23

3 Eighth-Day Christians:
   Living in God's Home Economics Project   47

4 The Catechism and the Ten Commandments:
   Law as the First Key to an Evangelical Design   73

5 The Catechism and Creed:
   Redemption as the Second Key to an Evangelical Design   101

6 The Catechism and the Lord's Prayer:
   The Kingdom of God as the Third Key to an Evangelical Design   117

7 Building Eighth-Day Disciples:
   Five More Foundational Keys for Mission and Ministry   133

8 Eighth-Day Discipleship in an Eight-Sided Church:
   Living by Faith with Responsibility and Freedom   149

   Study Guide   179
   Notes   189
   Selected Bibliography   199

Foreword

Though I was born in Montego Bay, Jamaica, I grew up in Hamilton, Ontario, the steel and metals manufacturing capital of Canada. Labour Day mattered. My family's Lutheran congregation also mattered. Confirmed there on Pentecost Sunday 1977, I was active in music and youth group. Though this was a vibrant community of faith, I don't recall hearing much correlation between the blue-collar, hard hat–wearing steelworkers in this gritty city and the city of God.

On most days, even the most faithful among us find ourselves moving at the speed of life, making our way on the day-to-day treadmill from duty to duty. Often reactive and reflexive, we are not necessarily reflective. Too many responsibilities and deadlines—shuttling kids to school and sports, getting pets to vets, adhering to calendar alerts, all worthy causes giving rise to worthwhile busyness, stressors and pressures demanding our attention—summon our attentiveness. In the face of all of this, we are masters of a skin-deep faith that often does not penetrate the heart of life's urgencies and exigencies. Yet life's myriad vocations have something intrinsically to do with faith, work, and economics.

Imagine an innovative, cross-cultural, forward-looking theologian, daring to offer a corresponding consideration: "The older we get, the more we need the catechism." Long before he was Rev. Dr. Richard Bliese, Rick was a typical pastor's kid. That means he endured plenty of opportunities for being drilled in Martin Luther's *Small Catechism*. Why more catechism? Bliese's admission permits us to trace beyond typical confirmation age the themes of faith, work, and economics latent in Luther's manual for discipleship. Even though Martin Luther's Ninety-Five Theses insists that the entire life of believers is one of repentance,[1] Lutherans and their theologians tend not to repent of their oversights. What Bliese missed was the lifelong, eighth-day discipleship dynamic that was there all along, hiding plainly in words he'd been reading, studying, praying, and teaching for nearly six decades.

Grounded in a catechetical ethos, Bliese walks us through his groundbreaking recognition. True recognition is to know something afresh based on previous experience with that phenomenon. Nothing nostalgic nor curmudgeonly marks Bliese's epiphany. It is drawn forth by a glimpse of an eighth-day eschatological vision made concrete for today. In retrospect, this should bring no surprise.

To use an architectural analogy, the church's theology is shaped by the biblical witness, but since God means for theology to be for life, those same pulsing theological priorities then shape the church. As Prosper of Aquitaine conjectured, *lex credendi* (the rule of faith) informs and is informed by *lex orandi* (the rule of prayer), both of which inform and are mutually informed by *lex vivendi* (the rule of living). Life works in a correlative tandem, circumscribing faith, work, and economics. To live healthily is not to be isolated or single-tiered, but to live interdependent, holistic, and integrated lives of full flourishing (*eudaimonia*).

The Bible's words about God's law and the gospel of promise are categories that form a hermeneutical home familiar to Bliese. The word of *God* comes first, according to Luther: "After it follows faith; after faith, love; then love does every good work, for . . . it is the fulfilling of the law."[2] This is not merely pedantic or academic for Bliese, whose journey finds faith through the "pain of unemploy-ment," through a summer farm job for which he was paid with a cow, and through missionary work in three continents, North America, Europe, and Africa.

Engaging with Bliese's work has prompted me to consider several takeaways missing in my own ministry (and perhaps others' in the church). For example,

- Can I find more creative and informed ways for my preaching to include workplace references and resources?
- Do I intentionally affirm the dignity of labor and nobility of laborers?

- How does my public witness express gratitude for essential workers?
- Do I visit the workplaces of church members and friends?

God's redemption in Christ encompasses intractable legal matters, thorny employment issues, budgetary challenges, and fundraising opportunities. These seemingly quotidian transactions form and are informed by faith, which leaks into life. Dividing Sunday's so-called spirituality from the so-called secularity of one's workweek cannot be attributed to Luther.

In the absence of healthy connections among faith, work, and economics, false ones arise. One heresy unmasked by Bliese, homegrown in the USA, is prosperity theology. Though productivity and labor ennoble people, enhance meaning in life, and benefit materially individuals and families, there is not an ironclad correlation between these things in an unjust and fallen world. Under the oppressive shadow of prosperity theology's half truths, being blessed is reduced to bodily health and material wealth.

People living in the desperation of socioeconomic poverty are prone to bad theologies that intensify poverty. When proof of God's favor is defined by an abundance of tangible possessions, these crooked conclusions are the result of flimsy theological architecture. For example, they ignore the implications of injustice. Scriptures and catechism warn us that possessions can be ill-gotten, as they are by those who "covet fields, and seize them; [desire] houses, and take them away; they oppress householder and house" (Mic 2:2). Poverty is multidimensional.

Ordinary Christian citizens in the ordinary places we live, love, work, play, and pray can construct meaningful and prophetic lives through Bliese's octagonal ordering of life: the birthplace of faith, in the eight-sidedness of the baptism's font, gains nurture in the eight sections of the catechism. This catechetical architecture orders our thinking about God while it connects the doctrinal dots to Christ's real presence in a broken world teeming with the Spirit's possibility.

Finally, this book also inspired this haiku prayer:

Faithful One, keep us
strong amid defeats and sins
till the eighth-day wins.

John Arthur Nunes
September 6, 2021
Labour Day 2021

Acknowledgments

Special thanks go to the Kern Family Foundation for generously supporting this project and offering the initial challenge to explore more deeply as Lutherans the three-legged stool of faith, work, and economics. I'm thankful for their vision.

Special appreciation goes to those people who have either taught or inspired me to reflect more deeply on matters of faith, work, and economics. Deep gratitude goes to my wife, Nina, who has regularly asked the encouraging question, "Are you working on the book today?" Other critical persons include Jack Fortin, Gary Moore, Jon Pahl, Gene Veith, Chris Armstrong, Jason Van Hunnik, Greg Forster, Wayne Miller, Phyllis Anderson, John Nunes, Stephanie Bliese, and David Housholder. The Made to Flourish network has played a strong role in numerous ways in deepening my appreciation for the biblical roots and nuance of this subject matter. Heartfelt appreciation to Tom Nelson and his team.

Finally, to the people of Emmanuel Lutheran Church in Naples, Florida, special thanks for participating in various congregational experiments around the topics of faith, vocation, and economics, as well as numerous issues surrounding Luther's *Small Catechism*. I wanted to write a book that could be read and studied within a community of faith. Thanks for being that community for me.

Introduction

An Evangelical Architecture for Eighth-Day Discipleship

Jesus's call, "Follow me," comes to us as a gift. This call is a call to discipleship, a call to live within a different day of the week. This gracious gift transforms us into a life within the most remarkable day of creation, the eighth day. The language of "the eighth day of creation" will sound new and strange at first. Nevertheless, this day's existence and dynamism lie at the heart of the New Testament's witness to Jesus Christ. This day of creation changes everything and makes all things new.

This remarkable understanding captured my imagination while touring early Christian sites in western Turkey and Greece. It was on this tour that I visited my first eight-sided church, the ancient basilica at Philippi. It was a beautiful archeological site, rich with religious history. The basilica's ruins sit high on a hill with panoramic views, blue sea far in the distance, and the countryside all around, still looking majestic on that ancient Roman road across Greece. My surprise came when I noticed this church's design. The church was an octagon; it had eight sides! I scratched my head in reflection. I hadn't remembered ever seeing an eight-sided church, or any eight-sided building, until that rainy afternoon. I climbed the hill and stood within the striking remains of this Byzantine-style basilica, asking the question, "Why eight sides?" I knew that various numbers had meanings within the Bible. But why had this Christian community chosen to be surrounded by *eight* walls?

Since that day in Greece, I have seen pictures of eight-sided churches all over the world. These octagonal buildings were not just built in the Byzantine era (the fourth through the fifteenth centuries CE). Churches have been built according to this eight-sided design in every era, in almost every culture, and across the entire world.[1]

But why?

That's what I wanted to know in 2012. The aesthetics of the design were beautiful. But I knew there must be a deeper religious meaning behind this specific form. If the old adage from Winston Churchill that "we shape buildings; thereafter they shape us" is true, then why did so many Christian communities throughout the ages choose an eight-sided architecture to shape and form them as disciples of Jesus?

"Early Christians," our guide explained, "were focused on God's new creation begun in Jesus, who rose from the dead on Sunday, the first day of the week. Instead of calling it the first day, however, these Christians understood resurrection as the continuation of God's creative activity. So the first day of the week became the eighth day of creation."

This young Greek guide had just gifted me with an important insight into the Bible story that I had overlooked in my many years of theological training. The eighth day of creation as a day of resurrection work! The day of discipleship!

AN ARCHITECTURE FOR DISCIPLESHIP

The eight-sided church provided an architectural metaphor for describing how to build a life of discipleship. Here, "architecture" means simply how you build, organize, or structure your life. Architecture is a marvelous way to describe the basic design elements of our faith life because the image is so tangible. The life of discipleship has a design and structure. You live in it. We all likely have some experience with good and bad architecture. We may know what it's like to live in a comfortable functional home or one that was designed poorly. We enjoy a home that is safe, and we suffer in homes that are not built well, that don't withstand cold, heat, or storms.

The life of discipleship functions the same way. Good spiritual architecture can inspire and elevate our spirits, provide safety in a storm and structure to our daily life. Solid spiritual buildings and foundations serve God's purposes for us: namely, that we thrive. This "thriving" includes our work and economic activities. It is no wonder that the New Testament uses an architectural metaphor to encourage us to build our lives not on the sand but on the rock (Matt 7:24–27).

Discipleship and architecture have always been expressed directly through church buildings. Architectural designs for churches have a huge effect on how people worship and understand the Christian life. The theology behind any church building is fascinating to explore.

The church building itself serves as a witness from and to the community. When constructing a church, the architect has many decisions to make. Should the altar face east? Is an altar needed at all? Is a steeple desired to lift high the cross as a witness in the neighborhood, or are bells employed to call to worship? Is the "sanctuary" traditional or more like a theater? Will a storefront design attract people from the neighborhood to worship? Is art important in focusing on the word of God, or does it distract from that very word? Pews or chairs? Stained glass or clear windows? Utilizing technology or deploying a classic design? Each decision is a theological statement, a witness and a confession of faith.

As I wrote this book, I watched the terrible destruction of one of the world's greatest architectural wonders, the Notre Dame Cathedral in Paris, France. As the flames rose high within that sacred space, so too did the gloom around the world. The signs of sadness were many and various. Some lamented the fire's assault on the beauty of the cathedral. Others mentioned the eight-hundred-year-old history of the church. Still others told personal stories about attending worship in this magnificent structure, admiring the translucent rose window or climbing its North tower.

Medieval cathedrals were built to create a theological vision, to preach and teach the faith. The building wasn't merely functional, designed as a place for worship. Much more was at stake! The whole architectural design of the cathedral told a larger story about God's activity in the world. The beauty of its whole architecture pointed to the ministry of Jesus and his message of redemption, pointing above all to the heavenly vision of "the New Jerusalem" found in the book of Revelation. The cathedral allowed the faithful to get a foretaste of the fruit of the kingdom described in the last book of the Bible. It inspired faithfulness in the present by painting a picture of the future. Christians could actually experience the future blessedness every time they stepped inside the walls of the cathedral. The future became present in that holy space. In 2019, a concrete expression of God's vision for the new creation had burned, not just a relic from the past.

It is with the metaphor of architecture then that the life of faith will be described. Building an architecture for living the faith has the same goal in mind as a medieval cathedral: namely, to paint a picture of God's activities in the world in which one can "live, breathe, and have meaning." I seek an architecture in which I can worship on Sunday and on Monday. My curiosity for a new approach to faith was tweaked through my own architectural discoveries in Greece and Turkey and on the campus of the University of Minnesota. The stories of these trips will be told in the next chapters. I find it fascinating now that architecture was the effective "teacher," not books. Architecture was the place where the penny dropped. Buildings prove to be good preachers.

Now is the time where we need good teachers, guides, builders, and architects. My conviction is that the separation of faith, work, and economics leads to poorly constructed lives of discipleship and struggling communities. Another way to summarize this separation is with the days of the week. Sunday and Monday are often experienced as separate, with no bridge between them. Human misery is the fruit of this divorce. This misery might begin with the individual, or it might begin with the community. Both suffer together in the end. This divorce between what happens on Sunday and Monday can negatively affect congregations because Christians are left vulnerable and exposed to the frequent economic storms of our times. Conversely, the integration of faith and economics leads to a path for human flourishing. This path takes seriously the call to discipleship in all areas of our lives. Without aligning faith, work, and economics, the call to follow Jesus will be irrational and irrelevant.

That is why I will emphasize the three ideas of faith, work, and economics as key design elements in building one's life of discipleship. Discipleship as architecture draws great insights from these three elements. I will also use this three-legged stool to go back and review my own spiritual heritage, the Reformation. Does the Reformation assist me in building a solid architecture for life today, or should I look for more modern ideas to build my house?

FAITH, WORK, AND ECONOMICS
AS KEY TOPICS FOR DISCIPLESHIP

Because these terms are critically important for reimagining Christian discipleship, let me define them right at the beginning.

Faith

Faith is understood as our response to a promise by God. Evangelical faith is our response to God's promise of the good news "for us" in Jesus Christ as Savior and Lord. I will expand this short definition more fully later by turning to Martin Luther's *Small Catechism*. Further, I make the claim that the *Small Catechism* defines faith as being evangelical. *Evangelical* here means "gospel-centered." I turn to Luther's *Small Catechism* because it has defined an evangelical faith for, now, over five hundred years. It may have been used to equip more Protestant Christians than any other discipleship manual in history.

Work

Work is part of the created order; it describes how we care for, preserve, and sustain our lives and the lives of our various communities. In addition, "work transforms this into that."[2] It creates. What is often forgotten, however, is that work is a response to God's various calls in our lives, whether we are Christian or not. This is the meaning of *vocation*. These calls or vocations are built into the very fabric of how God created humanity to function and thrive within communities. Work is baked into how God manages and stewards the world, down to the very last detail: for example, how a slice of bread ends up on my dinner plate or how a massive network of global businesses and distribution sites put an iPhone in my hand. Broadly defined, work involves much of our daily activities at home, at our places of employment, at school, in church, and within our neighborhoods. It may involve pay, but often it does not.

Economics

Economics is a rich word with various meanings—"stewardship," "management," "planning," "dispensation," and "mode of operation." I describe economics in three broad ways. First, it encompasses the big story of God's reign over the whole creation, a narrative that addresses the purpose and meaning of God's activity in the world. It's the Big Plan. Second, economics addresses the question of God's stewardship and management of creation. How does God manage the world? How does God steward creation? And how does God use humanity within this management and stewardship plan? Finally, my definition of economics explores the financial underpinnings of our lives and evaluates how our management of God's creation is working—or not working—and why. Economics involves assessment. Numbers tell a story and ground that story in reality.

THE ARCHITECTURE OF THIS BOOK

The number eight plays an important role throughout this book. The book is designed like an eight-sided building. (I introduced the meaning of eight-sided churches at the beginning, and I will explain this concept more fully in the following chapters.) The number eight has particular significance here because it refers to new life and resurrection. Eight chapters were used therefore to emphasize this theme. Eight elements of Luther's *Small Catechism* will also be employed: the Ten Commandments, the Apostles' Creed, the Lord's Prayer, baptism, communion, confession (otherwise known as the Office of the Keys), blessings, and the Table of Duties.

The first three chapters, plus the introductory chapter, use architecture and various personal stories to connect faith, work, and economics. Since these topics might be unfamiliar, much energy has been spent on setting up a solid foundation for the conversation. After setting the stage by establishing the lenses of faith, work, and economics for framing discipleship, chapters 4, 5, 6, and 7 will explore the eight dimensions of Luther's *Small Catechism* to see how and where faith, work, and economics play a role in this classic description of evangelical faith rooted in the Reformation. Chapter 8 summarizes the practical fruits of these explorations.

For disciples of Jesus, work should always be understood in light of a larger story. The larger picture clarifies and motivates both the work and the worker. A boss wants to know if a worker—any worker, from top to bottom—fits into the larger picture of the organization's mission. Therefore, we turn now to that larger picture of God's mission as it clarifies the divine importance of our everyday labors.

1

Building Discipleship to Withstand Economic Storms

"There is no such thing as a truly free market; all freedom is obedience to something. A Protestant ethic (or ethics) is neither essentially capitalist nor anti-capitalist; it is pro-freedom, insofar as freedom enables individuals and communities to love their neighbors as themselves."

Kathryn D. Blanchard in
The Protestant Ethic or The Spirit of Capitalism

Before I return to exploring the remarkable eighth day and the discipleship it engenders, I want us to step back and consider how God's people are often called to eighth-day discipleship in the midst of storms, particularly work-related and economic storms and issues related to personal wealth and its use.

In 1970, the Apollo 13 mission to the moon began without a hitch, but this historic trip was cut short when a sudden explosion onboard crippled the ship. The dramatic event was immortalized in the famous words of astronaut Jack Swigert, who calmly acknowledged the awful reality of the crew's plight: "Houston, we have a problem."[1] In the movie named after the mission, we see fear build as family and friends and NASA engineers grasp the gravity of the situation. What if the astronauts cannot fix the problem? Will the crew be stuck in space forever? Was their training adequate for the challenge? How do people respond when faced with life-threatening conditions? Tension builds as the astronauts try to solve the problem together with the anxious but skilled technicians at the NASA Mission Control Center.

When Hurricane Harvey hit Texas in 2017, Swigert's famous quote took on new meaning. Hurricane Harvey wreaked havoc on the city of Houston, dumping trillions of gallons of water on this Gulf Coast city where sixty-eight people died, leaving, by one estimate, $125 billion of damage in its wake. Homes were flooded, and some were destroyed. The simple fact is that many houses in and around Houston were not built to withstand that kind of weather onslaught. Building a home to withstand a category-five hurricane is, after all, expensive. Many people had accepted the risks of living in inadequate housing. Like astronauts in space, therefore, they accepted certain dangers. They hoped those dangers would never materialize. Unfortunately, calamity struck. Over twenty-five thousand households were displaced.[2]

WHAT KIND OF HOUSE DO I NEED?

What has been the response to these storms? The short answer from Houstonians has been a resolute one: "We must build better homes." This is good advice. After the multiple floods since 2014, local officials have developed rules for rebuilding homes in flood-prone areas. Residents must now seriously think through what can withstand category-five hurricanes if they want to rebuild their homes in Houston. These officials are making more stringent architectural demands for multiple reasons, because above all, indifference to change will prove costly for everyone.

Residents and families must invest in building better homes and neighborhoods. As everyone knows, the hurricanes will come again. Weather patterns suggest that floods will regularly threaten Houston. Most people love their homes. They love their neighborhoods. They love their schools and friends. They love Houston! Despite so much love, the status quo of housing is no longer sustainable. As one resident confessed, "Honestly, I wish we were rebuilding higher."[3]

BUILDING CHRISTIAN DISCIPLESHIP THAT LASTS

Since moving to Florida, I have experienced firsthand the dangers of hurricane season. The threat is real. You must live in a well-built home or take your chances every hurricane season.

The life of discipleship requires careful construction as well, especially as Christians face the regular boom-and-bust cycles of daily work and the present economy. Nearly everyone has experienced these economic realities. One minute you have a good job, the next minute you don't. One day you can afford health insurance, the next day you can't. If you are a two-person-income household, the same job insecurity applies to your spouse as well. Without two good jobs, many families can't make it financially. Furthermore, the speed of economic change increases the feelings of insecurity. Some argue that these dynamics are just part and parcel of our capitalistic system. The advice you receive from well-meaning friends can prove to be enervating, especially if you face job insecurity.

As I was looking for work a few years ago, one good friend gave me a self-help book for job seekers called *What Color Is Your Parachute?*[4] His counsel to me was, "Having to change jobs regularly is just the way our economy works, so adjust your life accordingly." His advice was clear, "There is no job security. Sorry. That's life."

Who hasn't felt the queasiness of this economic roller-coaster ride or gazed fearfully at the storm clouds of these existential threats? I have. One day, I was the president of a large Lutheran seminary; two weeks later, I was "resigned." A crisis emerged at the school. I wasn't blamed—directly. Nevertheless, I was the president. I was responsible. The board decided a change was required. The decision came suddenly. No warning was given. No explanation. No deliberations. All of a sudden, a decision was made. I had lost my job. Questions of identity and purpose began to swirl around my life. Why did this happen? How will I support my family? Am I still valued in the community?

Studies by economists in England and Australia point out a painful reality: it often takes longer to adapt to the pain of unemployment than to losing a loved one.[5] At first, this statement appears jarring. Nevertheless, data backs up the brutal effects that both losses can inflict on a person's life. Being fired or unemployed is devastating. Why? Because so much of our self-esteem, identity, and purpose in life are tied tightly together with our daily work.

Sudden job loss is a common experience today. Job security is rare. "Adaptability" is preached, even in the church. Pastors understand this vulnerability. Which church leader doesn't fear that they are just one bad budget cycle, one disgruntled donor, or one season of weak attendance away from a "new call." In addition, ever since 2020, people ask how biological storms, such as a virus or pandemic, might affect their work, their personal economies, or their vocations.

The reality of ministry performance is that it is measured in part by budgets and attendance. But how much adaptability can a business, church, family, or individual bear as those measurements regularly fluctuate? And whom does constant and perennial "adaptability" serve in the final analysis? When work and personal identity are so tightly braided together, job loss creates fundamental questions about life. Those fundamental questions are now asked regularly in every home.

The church and those who serve the church are not immune from economic storms, of course. That's because churches are made up of everyday people living on Main Street, and the economic ups and downs of Main Street can be extremely volatile. Jobs now come and go quickly, and often without any relationship to job performance. Companies "downsize" or "rightsize" the business when "the market demands it." What do you do when the pink slip comes under your door, or the board decides your career is done because the market says so?

In response to this constant aura of vulnerability, people around the world sense that the market's need for constant "creative destruction" is hard to bear. Something is fundamentally wrong with how we have built our economic lives as individuals and as a community. The critiques abound and are growing, and some of them will be described later. The key is that someone or something has thrown a monkey wrench into the system. We sense it on a macro level. Our politicians debate its *causes* now, not its *existence*. Economists argue about solutions. CEOs wrestle with their responsibility, caught between the health of their employees and the health of their companies.

We all experience this raw economic vulnerability in our personal lives at ground zero, around kitchen tables, and with neighbors in our communities. The threatening dark clouds hover ominously overhead. Heavy winds loom large. Destruction awaits. That's our fear, at least. Experts describe this economic dynamic as "creative destruction." Yes, there is some creativity for "the economy" here. Let's admit it. But let's not overlook either the destruction to real people, such as those sixty-year-old workers who just lost their jobs to people on the other side of the planet. Or the college graduate who simply can't enter the economy in any meaningful way. Houston, we have a problem.

WHY ARE THESE WORK-RELATED QUESTIONS SO IMPORTANT?

These metaphors of category-five storms and pandemics are being used within this context for two reasons. First: our work and the economy dominate much of our lives. They shape us and our families in powerful ways. When your personal economy is doing well, that one fact makes a huge difference in your entire life for your education, health, nutrition, education, marriage and family, and personal well-being. This dynamic also holds true for neighborhoods and whole communities. One more point: a good economy also affects your spiritual life.

Second, given how important economic issues are for our well-being and the well-being of our family members, it is shocking that we don't speak much about the topics of faith, work, and economics at church. We don't even talk much about money. It's as if we are living in Houston before 2017—that is, we know the storms are coming, but we simply let people build in dangerous neighborhoods and construct their homes in any way they desire. A laissez-faire lifestyle is the result. Financial hurricanes are striking our neighborhoods more frequently now. These economic storms disrupt lives. In response, shockingly, the church often says as little as possible about money, jobs, finances, business, or the economy. Sometimes we do offer prayers, but usually after the destruction has passed. "Thoughts and prayers" plus funerals are the church's specialty.

Why is it that many congregations fall silent in the face of economic storms? Do we know what to say or do? Think of the single mother who comes to church regularly but suddenly loses her steady employment. With two small children, the job was her lifeline. She turns to her pastor, to her Bible study friends, and to her fellow parents in the nursery. What should they say? What can they realistically do? Praying for this mother is important, but does the prayer then lead to action? How does the call to eighth-day discipleship intersect with the economic realities of our lives? As communities of faith, how do we build expertise and empathy to deal with economic subjects, let alone economic storms? One thing is certain: economic issues challenge Christians on Monday in fundamental ways. What we say on Sunday needs to prepare people for these storms. Any Christian community that imagines serving the neighbor must consider their work lives. Eighth-day discipleship embraces talking about economics and imagines faith in the context of this conversation.

We need to explore the critical relationship among faith, our work, and economics in the church. Many people aren't prepared for the big economic storms in life, and maybe not even the smaller ones. Many Christians suffer economic hardships without the benefit of Christian teaching or the direct support of their local faith community. Sunday and Monday have become divorced. The consequences of the split have brought grave consequences to regular people—that is, to people we know and those neighborhoods we love.

THE "STORM" OF CORONAVIRUS

As I was writing this book, the pandemic of the coronavirus had just struck the United States with full force. Martin Luther, in his famous Reformation hymn "A Mighty Fortress," referred to an epidemic in

Wittenberg as "hordes of devils fill[ing] the land." Viruses work their evil plans like demons of old, invisible yet deadly. Covid-19 looks for weaknesses to exploit.

The pandemic's devastation has surfaced health-related concerns as well as economic issues at all levels of our nation, from the president at the top to all "essential workers." Everyone debates how to balance health, safety, and the economy. These questions go to the heart of how we define the nature of human life, human thriving, and human community. One little virus has turned the world upside down.

Much like the hurricane in Houston, the economic roller coaster following the pandemic has been on full display every night on the news. Within a two-week period in February 2020, the US economy went from being "strong and robust" (with unemployment below 3.5 percent and Wall Street making record profits) to being a wasteland. US economic numbers sank to levels not seen since the Great Depression. Technically, a bear market occurs when we have a drop of 20 percent or more from a peak. Historically, it has taken an average of eight months for a market to enter bear territory. From February 19 to March 12, 2020, the S&P 500 fell by about 27 percent. We entered a bear market in less than a month. That's the fastest drop ever.

How do we respond to economic upheaval in the lives of our families and our nation? How can our faith help us frame the economic and work challenges we face every day?

TALKING ABOUT ECONOMICS

Everyone knows how important work and economics are for daily life. They dominate talk around the kitchen table, in the office, at school, at local clubs, and in the marketplace. So why are many congregations so reluctant to engage in these conversations?

There is no simple answer to this important question. But one initial response has begun to convince me: The local congregation has gladly and willingly punted the ball. Local congregations don't want to own the responsibility for these "secular" issues. The church has simply allowed other groups and worldviews to carry the ball, so to speak, in informing and teaching about the importance of our work and economic lives. If clergy rarely mention these topics in sermons or Bible studies, people conclude that the gospel doesn't speak to these subjects. Sometimes the message reduces the gospel to an individual's heart, shrinking "good news" to the internal matters of the soul. In so doing, we give away the responsibility for "external" or "secular" matters to other worldviews, political parties, economists, or clever pundits. How quickly we feign helplessness and let these alternative voices do the heavy lifting.

American Christianity has been subtly "colonized" by worldviews that have either degraded Christian teaching or jettisoned it altogether. This colonization leads to families suffering and people's lives being damaged. These alternative worldviews leave Christians vulnerable when facing all kinds of storms, especially when these storms come with economic consequences.

Why have we allowed this to happen? Although these alternative worldviews may be a cheap substitute for the genuine article, they do claim to provide expertise on how to improve our Monday lives. They are pragmatic. Some experts even claim to link spirituality with their self-help advice. The result is this: if the church cannot or will not provide what is needed, people go shopping elsewhere. Houston, we have a problem!

Which worldviews are replacing the gospel? These alternative voices will be explored more fully below. For now, however, I will argue that these worldviews encourage families, workers, students, and businesspeople to build, as it were, inadequate houses on land vulnerable to frequent storms. They ignore commonsense protections against spiritual viruses. Bad construction and inadequate planning are now also true for the church as it practices discipleship. Sand makes for weak foundations.

As a Christian leader, I have recently come to realize that I am a part of the problem. Have I, in effect, been allowing my people, however unwittingly, to build their spiritual lives today like the homes in Houston before 2017? Am I helping them withstand, so to speak, the economic pandemics that have come and those that will come again? I would love to consider myself a prophet for change. But honestly, a prophet for change doesn't settle for a laissez-faire approach to Christian discipleship.

THE ALTERNATIVE WORLDVIEWS

Here, then, is a look at those worldviews that are filling in the gap left by the church's silence. Caution: these worldviews are seductive.

In my view, four prominent worldviews have emerged in our communities, each attempting to provide a viable way to prepare people for the roller-coaster ride of life. To be absolutely clear, these worldviews aren't Christian, although they often dress up like it. They serve up thin soup for the soul. They are inadequate to build one's life as a follower of Jesus, but they do have massive sway within congregations. Parents will often pass on these worldviews to their children. They can prove attractive. This is because we learn these worldviews at home, in school, in the office, and at the store. Our friends promote these ideals. Movies promote their allure from the big screen and our computers. They are in the cultural air that we breathe. The four worldviews are

1. moralistic therapeutic deism as a *religious* worldview;
2. capitalism as a *moral* worldview (*homo economicus*);
3. the prosperity gospel as a *spiritual* worldview; and
4. tribalism as a *cultural* and *spiritual* worldview.

Let's briefly describe each of these and its impact on Christian discipleship.

Moralistic Therapeutic Deism

Moralistic therapeutic deism claims that God wants us to be happy. Happiness is the ultimate goal of life. If we're good people and nice to our neighbors and the environment, God will reward us first with happiness and then with heaven. Christian Smith describes this worldview well in his book *Soul Searching*, where he explores the religious beliefs of young adults and their parents. He writes,

We have come with some confidence to believe that a significant part of Christianity in the U.S. is actually only tenuously
Christian in any sense that is seriously connected to the actual
historical Christian tradition but has rather substantially mor-
phed into Christianity's misbegotten step cousin, Christian
Moralistic Therapeutic Deism. This has happened in the minds
and hearts of many believers and, it also appears, in the structures of at least some Christian organizations and institutions.
The language, and therefore experience, of Trinity, holiness,
sin, grace, justification, sanctification, church, Eucharist, and
heaven and hell appear, among most Christian teenagers in the
U.S. at the very least, to be supplanted by the language of happiness, niceness, and an earned heavenly reward. It is not so
much that U.S. Christianity is being secularized. Rather more
subtly, Christianity is either degenerating into a pathetic version of itself or, more significantly, Christianity is actively being
colonized and displaced by quite different religions.[6]

Capitalism

A second worldview is capitalism as a *moral* worldview, not just as
an economic system. The point here is not to start a debate comparing various economic theories. Rather, it is to recognize that our
economic theories are now functioning like rivers that overrun their
banks, influencing everything in life. Economics isn't staying within
its lane. While pretending to be morally neutral, our capitalistic system functions quite openly in promoting its own ethics and morality.
It assigns value to everything around us, even personal relationships
and our religious life.

Again, Christian Smith recognizes the effect of economics and
consumerism on young adults:

In fact, however, American religion and spirituality, including
teenagers' involvement in them, may be profoundly shaped by
American mass-consumer capitalism. Capitalism is not merely a

system for the efficient production and distribution of goods and services; it also incarnates and promotes a particular moral order, and institutionalized normative worldview comprising and fostering particular assumptions, narratives, commitments, beliefs, values, and goals. Capitalism not only puts food on the table, it also powerfully defines for those who live in it in elemental terms both what is and what should be, however taken for granted those definitions ordinarily may be.[7]

We will refer to the harmful use of economics as a moral system as *homo economicus*. Don't let the Latin word fool you. It's a funny name but it's a real thing on Wall Street *and* Main Street.

The Prosperity Gospel

Third, the prosperity gospel as a *spiritual* worldview builds on our desire to thrive by gaining God's favor. In our North American culture, we are surrounded by messages about prosperity. Prosperity is packed into our advertisements, our media, the marketplace, and our neighborhoods. In response, our desire to prosper can grow either like a flower or like a weed. Most economic worldviews are presented to us as "secular," but the prosperity gospel depends on God to deliver prosperity. The goal of this worldview is to invest in God so that God will invest in us. Seeds of faith are planted to win God's favor. These transactions function like a contract. Notice the "if, then" quality of this contract. If you do this, then God will do that. The faithful are encouraged to sacrifice financially to show how real and serious their commitments to God really are. The more these "seeds of faith" are planted, with checks written as proof, the better chance a person has of God honoring the promise to grant them prosperity. It's transactional. God will bless those who are faithful with wealth and prosperity. But what happens when prosperity does not follow faith and sacrificial giving? The prosperity gospel is not a helpful building block for real discipleship.

Tribalism

Finally, in a scary world, it is always tempting to retreat into some form of tribalism. Tribalism is cultural in nature and quite powerful. The dynamic of tribalism's allure appears at times like religious zeal. Desiring some form of group cohesion comes naturally to us as social beings, of course. Belonging to a tribe can prove to be healthy. Family, nation, church, class, ethnic group, club, sports team, local community—all provide sources of comfort and stability. This is true unless these groups are weaponized against other tribes. Once your tribe has become weaponized, then it takes precedence over the words of Jesus. Your tribe becomes a form of idolatry. In such a tribe, you cannot love or serve the neighbor, especially if that neighbor belongs to a rival gang. Empathy is discouraged. Walls are constructed and justified, at times even misusing the Bible as a prop. Racism functions this same way. Nationalism too. They pit one Christian against another and one human against another, claiming God as their patron.

Christian churches sometimes turn to tribalism, allowing their members to disparage other churches, religions, ethnic groups, and even other individual Christians. History is replete with such stories. German troops marched into World War II wearing a tribal message on their belts: "God with us." This was a bold statement, since their enemies in World War II also claimed to be Christian.

As a Lutheran, I can still remember the anti-Catholic rantings I heard in my youth. Catholics lived one way as a religious tribe, and Lutherans lived another. We were taught that these divisions were "righteous." Both sides seemed content with this intertribal warfare. Naturally, God was on our Lutheran side, we declared, because we preached the "true gospel." That's how disorienting tribalism can be. God's call to unity (John 17) can be easily discarded without a second thought.

The bottom line is that people won't be prepared for the storms in their lives if they substitute any of the four worldviews for real Christian discipleship.[8] Congregations need to identify and talk about these rivals. Economic storms destabilize lives built on these alternative voices. Local congregations have been largely quiet about these rival worldviews and their inadequacy to withstand the big storms that have come. Sunday and Monday have become divorced at the worst possible moment.

HOW YOU BUILD YOUR LIFE

Reading about the architectural changes required in Houston so that buildings could withstand future storms has forced me to reflect on the importance of architecture in structuring spiritual lives of discipleship. I love architecture. Entering a beautifully designed building always gives me a rush.

I remember the excitement I experienced on my first trip to Disney World. My high school madrigal group was invited to sing on the Fantasy Fair stage at Disney World in Orlando in 1972. To be honest, I don't remember our performance. What captured my imagination was the amazing atmosphere at Disney World. Each separate village or section of the park had its own music, its own costumes, and its own architectural theme. Furthermore, no two sections of the park overlapped. Each area was designed to elicit certain feelings and emotions from the guests. These designs worked for me at fifteen! They still do.

The point is that as you enter any space, its architecture affects you in fascinating ways. The emotions stir. Your eyes widen. You explore every detail, even if only unconsciously. Feelings start to bubble up inside you, be they peaceful feelings, delight, or a sense of well-being. Other feelings might arise too: curiosity and puzzlement, displeasure, or even disease. The whole body is engaged because you are completely wrapped up and affected by the aesthetics of your environment. Good architecture can elevate the spirit.

A building's design also organizes life within it. Form and function work best when they are successfully married. We experience this every day in our homes, schools, and offices. Your daily routines change depending on how rooms are structured. A building's size, floor design, lighting, plumbing, and square footage matter. Does the form of the house or office space serve the function of a family's life or someone's work life? A thousand design decisions come together in constructing a building. All architectural decisions are made so that people thrive in a given space, so that life functions smoothly and appropriately there.

Finally, a good architectural design builds a structure that can withstand the elements outside. These "elements" usually involve cold and rain, snow and ice, sun and wind, animals big and small, and more. If you live on the Gulf Coast, for example, the "elements" involve category-five hurricanes and lots of small bugs. An architectural design today that doesn't take these threats seriously is irresponsible.

The principal point here is that an architect builds a structure where form and function work together so that the family home, business, or school can thrive. Architecture, no matter how simple or complex, must serve the people who live, work, or play in it.

This is the danger of worldviews that conflict with the Christian gospel. These alternative worldviews promise people an integration of spirituality, work, and economics, but they can't deliver on that promise. When storms come, these voices leave people vulnerable and exposed.

We cannot talk about a full understanding of eighth-day discipleship without taking into account the economic realities of our lives, which are defined by both challenges and opportunities. Our faith may be tested by economic challenges. But discipleship also challenges us to grasp the big story of God's economy and our call to be stewards of that economy, including serving those most vulnerable to economic hardship.

Next, I want to turn to another aspect of the architecture of eighth-day discipleship by exploring the fundamental and fascinating connection between faith and work.

2

Connecting Faith
and Work

A Christian is a perfectly free lord of all, subject to none. A
Christian is a perfectly dutiful servant of all, subject to all.
—Martin Luther, *On Christian Liberty*

I have been making the case for the importance of integrating faith,
work, and economics within the call to discipleship. This threefold
integration represents good architecture for building a life of faith.
But when these three critical dimensions of discipleship are neglected,
other voices emerge to fill the gaps. In this chapter, I want to dwell
more deeply on the relationship between faith and work. Three bold
assertions will kick off the discussion:

1. Work is important to God.

The first stories in the Bible make this clear! But let's be more specific:

2. *Your* work is important to God.

Do you actually truly believe this amazing assertion? But let's up the
ante by making an even bolder assertion about *your* work:

3. Your work matters with how God manages the world. In
   other words, God is loving the world through you and your
   work.

Most Christians don't know these basic biblical assertions. They might even doubt them at first blush. Why does God need me? Yet these assertions rest at the core of God's plan for all creation. They are essential to the gospel itself. Unfortunately, they seem too grandiose to be true, at least when people reflect on their normal, everyday work lives. Imagine, though, if these assertions were true. If they were, in fact, biblical, they would change everything about how Christians approach their workweek—that is, how *you* approach your daily work.

A HISTORY OF WORK

Many Christians never think about how their work connects to their faith. In fact, Sunday's faith experiences are often segregated from Monday's work. A short historical review reveals how many of our attitudes about work are inherited from other cultures, especially the Greeks. Most ancient cultures had a low view of manual labor, saving high praise only for the "favored" life of aristocrats, nobility, and military generals. The Greeks acknowledged some value in work, especially farm labor. But the value of menial labor with one's hands paled in comparison to the life that incorporated philosophy, the arts, music, and culture. Leisure time reflected good fortune and the gods' favor because it allowed a person to follow the contemplative life. As a result, Greek life was designed around the many serving the few; servants, slaves, and workers in the lower socioeconomic positions supported the contemplative lives of the elite.[1]

Medieval spirituality kept this Greek distinction largely in place, referring to this dual tract as the "contemplative life" and the "active life." Each had its place in society, but the contemplative life reflected a higher spirituality and was thus chosen by most priests and monks. True discipleship was defined by the clergy. Their vows of chastity, poverty, and obedience wedded them to the higher demands of God outlined in the Sermon on the Mount while the common worker was given lower standards. As "workers" they were "merely" to follow the Ten Commandments.

Although few Protestants today would use these terms to describe the dual nature of work and spirituality, attitudes toward work have remained remarkably similar down through the ages. Many Christians still think of church work or ministry as holy work. In contrast, business and family life are viewed as routine, mundane, and even secular. Many Christians imagine that evangelism is truly God's work. At the same time, they are not sure about the divine character of car repair, retail sales, and secretarial work, just to name a few vocations. Common, everyday work seems too "normal" and too messy to be spiritual, especially when money, monotonous chores, or the secular marketplace are involved.

The imagined separation between the secular and sacred is further reinforced by the four Gospels, in which Jesus calls his disciples away from their families and work—away from their nets, daily labor, or tax collecting—into a life of discipleship. True spirituality, it is assumed, means leaving everything "earthly" behind to follow Jesus.

This false reading of the "call narratives" and the resulting lower view of daily work is exactly what Martin Luther questioned at the time of the Reformation. In one of his most famous works, *The Babylonian Captivity of the Church*, he writes, "Therefore I advise no one to enter any religious order or the priesthood, indeed, I advise everyone against it, unless he is forearmed with this knowledge and understands that the works of monks and priests, however holy and arduous they may be, do not differ one whit in the sight of God from the works of the rustic laborer in the field or the woman going about her household tasks, but that all works are measured before God by faith alone."[2]

WORKING INSIDE A DIVINE STORY

So how can any person regain a spiritual understanding of daily work? One key is to focus on the role of "story." Work is never just about "work." Our work is always embedded within a story. The story we tell about our work—or the story that is chosen for us—is critical. As we will discover later, work defined in Scripture belongs within the grand story of God's redemptive activity in the world. God's work and our work are intertwined right from the beginning.

People tell stories about their work to explain its significance or lack of significance. The stories you use to describe work and daily activities matter for how you understand the meaning of these things. These stories pull the pieces about your daily life together into a compelling overarching narrative. To understand your work, therefore, you must understand the stories in which your work is wrapped.

One special person who embodied for me how faith and work live within stories was Maryland dairy farmer Marge Street. As an eleven-year-old boy, I was asked to work all summer on Mrs. Street's large dairy farm in Blenheim, Maryland, just north of Towson. My father was the pastor of Saint John's, the local Lutheran Church–Missouri Synod. Mrs. Street was one of the church's most faithful members. I was a big boy at age eleven and athletic, so Mrs. Street approached my mother with an attractive offer. She would invite me to join her farmhands for the summer. She explained to my parents that I would not be compensated with money. Rather I would be given a heifer at the end of the summer as payment and be responsible for taking care of the animal. With four young boys at home, my mother gratefully accepted the offer. For my part, I had to drop my summer dreams of baseball fields in favor of cornfields. I would later come to appreciate the time on the farm as one of the most formative summers of my life.

Mrs. Street (Marge to her friends) was larger than life. Her laugh was infectious. So too was her faith. When Marge talked about the farm, she talked about her faith. It seemed natural for her. On her office desk, the Bible was usually open alongside financial documents from the farm. The same was true for the Bible on her nightstand. Her husband teased her about her multiple Bibles: "Shouldn't one Bible be sufficient for a person?" Marge's farmwork was God's work. Plowing the fields was a divine call "to be fruitful"; Marge often quoted from Genesis 1 and 2. She knew she was doing God's work with the soil on behalf of the community.

What is it about farming and putting your fingers into the soil that creates organic connections between faith and work? What was the larger story that gave Marge Street's work meaning? This story was God's creation story; in it, she heard God's call for her to work the land and feed the community. Marge Street is a strong example of a "faith-filled" storyteller. Ask Marge about things "down on the farm," and she would tell an economic story with numbers attached to gallons of milk sold, calves born, pounds of potatoes produced, leases on land and new farm equipment, all wrapped in the affirmation of God's call and blessings. Marge's faith came packaged in farm stories, manure and all!

To test the relationship between story and work, just ask any successful business owner to talk about their business. Sit down with a cup of coffee and be prepared to listen. The same dynamic holds true for families. Once the conversation touches on "work," it spreads out into many dimensions of a person's life. Are they feeling fulfilled? Is their career on the right path? Are they making enough money to make ends meet? Are their work life and family life balanced? How is their parenting going? The bottom line is this: stories tell us about the meaning of our work, and they often involve numbers. The divine dimension of each of these stories is usually not hidden. God is in the numbers.

At the end of the day, this is the essential role that economists play. Rather than being the oft-quoted "dismal science," economics tells tales. Economists are storytellers. Storytellers with numbers. What distinguishes work-related stories from other kinds of narratives is that they contain red-and-black ink, "bottom lines." Work-related stories contain lots of details: numbers and graphs, statistics and ratios, specialized equations and logarithms, and even prophetic projections about the future. These stories touch family budgets, paychecks, bank loans, mortgages, career choices, educational opportunities, work opportunities, health care choices, risks and rewards, and all kinds of kitchen table issues. Our economies tell stories about how life is working for us. Or how life might be broken. Are we being "fruitful"? Put in spiritual terms, numbers will tell a story of whether we are thriving—and whether we are thriving according to God's will. Beyond this, we should ask, Is our neighbor or our neighborhood thriving? Numbers reveal critical plots and story lines in our families, communities, cities, and places of work. Here we discover, again and again, that God is in those numbers. But where? We will come back to this critical question. Much hangs in the balance of how we discern and discover God in our work-related stories.

AS AN ECONOMIST, YOU ARE A STORYTELLER

Economists truly believe in the power of stories, even if they are taught to hide their story lines behind "neutral" numbers and graphs.[3] But numbers also give a story deeper roots in reality. Consequently, in your home and in your work life, you play the role of a storyteller. When it comes to your work, you are an economist.

My grandparents loved to tell stories about how they survived during the Great Depression. These stories seemed so foreign to me as a child, though today they seem contemporary and relevant. As they told us these tales, they always included certain key numbers that gave meaning to their various forms of work. For example, my grandparents loved to tell us about their childhood work. Grandpa described the meager cents per day he earned as a kid on paper routes. Grandma sold lemonade on the street corner. As adults, they shared how much they lost when the banks in Rockford, Illinois, collapsed. They explained how much a loaf of bread cost them in 1937 and how much they earned at the factory in 1938. Their stories were peppered with these details both during and after World War II. These stories were laden with values gleaned from tough times. Nothing meant more to my grandparents than "an honest day's work" and genuine gratitude for God's blessings.

On the other hand, numbers can be used to lie; as Mark Twain famously quipped, "There are three kinds of lies: lies, damned lies, and statistics."[4] Consequently, economists are storytellers, whether the economist is you, your spouse, your CFO, a local politician, or Adam Smith. Sometimes, as amateur economists, our storytelling is good, and sometimes it is bad. How we use numbers makes all the difference in how we tell our stories and what meaning we give to our daily work. Whether it's the truth or lies.

Quoting two economists, Tomáš Sedláček affirms the power of story within economics: "The human mind is built to think in terms of narratives . . . in turn, much of human motivation comes from living through a story of our lives, a story that we tell ourselves and that creates a framework of our motivation. Life could be just 'one damn thing after another'[5] if it weren't for such stories. . . . Great leaders are foremost creators of stories."[6] He goes on to say,

> All of economics is, in the end, economics of good and evil. It is the telling of stories by people of people to people. Even the most sophisticated mathematical model is, de facto, a story, a parable, our effort to (rationally) grasp the world around us. I will try to show that to this day that story, told through economic mechanisms, is essentially about a "good life," a story we have borne from the ancient Greek and Hebrew traditions. . . . People today, as they have always, want to know from economists principally what is good and what is bad.[7]

LOOKING FOR A STORY TO DESCRIBE OUR ECONOMY

We need our stories about work and economics to transcend materialistic measurements. We all need stories that aren't just about "paying the bills" or self-interested accumulation of wealth. Work gives meaning and purpose to our lives. Therefore, we need to think creatively about how society organizes and values work. And weaponizing terms such as *socialists* or *capitalists* to argue ideologically with others is not useful. When it comes to talking about work today, to quote Shakespeare in the play *Hamlet*, "Something is rotten in the state of Denmark." Something about the story doesn't ring true. Critiques of our present approach to profits, losses, and "self-interest" as the central focus of business, work, and labor are growing.

In the *Economist*, we read, "The West must find a way of putting individual initiative, the necessary driving-force of progress, within a shaping moral order. . . . Otherwise, the history books will record that the people of the West woke up during the 21st Century to discover that the pursuit of efficiency was not the same as the achievement of a happy life. The West, they will say, found itself living in a superbly efficient but, in the end, aimless machine."[8]

Rod Dreher, author of *The Benedict Option*, writes, "What has been missing from capitalism for a long time is any sense of morality, care for the neighbor and community, and love for the 'other' that Christianity absolutely demands, but that this current iteration of capitalism says is foolish. . . . I began to wonder what, exactly, mainstream conservatism was conserving. It dawned on me that some of the causes championed by my fellow conservatives—chiefly an uncritical enthusiasm for the market—can in some circumstances undermine the thing that I, as a traditionalist, considered the most important institution to conserve: the family."[9]

From the Roman Catholic tradition, Pope Francis expresses the critique more pointedly when he says, "The system's gangrene cannot be whitewashed forever."[10] He has even described the present global economy as "pathological."[11]

What is remarkable is that business leaders are also recognizing the importance of returning to a healthy economy and work based on more than shareholder value. For example, the Business Roundtable, a group of chief executive officers—nearly two hundred CEOs of nearly two hundred US companies—recently issued a statement with a new definition of the "purpose of a corporation."[12] Instead of the previous definition, which focused solely on shareholders and maximizing their profits, these leaders call on corporations to

- invest in their employees,
- deliver value to their customers,
- deal ethically with suppliers,
- deal ethically with their customers,
- provide guidance on social and moral issues, and
- support their outside communities.[13]

So now the conscience of Wall Street is taking center stage. What a reversal! The memories of Wall Street greed from the 1980s, and the "greed is good" character of Gordon Gekko from the movie *Wall Street*, are still fresh in our memories. Jamie Dimon, chairman and CEO of JPMorgan Chase and chairman of the Business Roundtable, was quoted in 2019 as saying, "The American dream is alive, but fraying. Major employers are investing in their workers and communities because they know it is the only way to be successful over the long term. These modernized principles reflect the business community's unwavering commitment to continue to push for an economy that serves all Americans."[14]

What is remarkable is that some of the most "prophetic" voices that are exposing the economic story as unsustainable come from the business community.

ECONOMICS AND WORK

These prophets are the watchers on the wall calling us back to an economic story that reflects a grander vision of humanity, community, and work. The prophets have been crying out for years both inside and outside the church! Talking about economic matters in such lofty ways leads us back to work. Daily work. Your daily work. Let's get personal. How do you understand the character and purpose of your work? Certainly, work serves a higher purpose than serving a financial bottom line. It's good when it puts bread on the table. But does your work mean more?

The essential value of work has become particularly evident during the coronavirus pandemic. Jobs once viewed as "simple," "manual labor" or "low-level employment," became "essential" overnight. It was not only doctors, nurses, and police officers who became highly valued in our society. In our war with the virus, grocers, meat packers, food deliverers, truck drivers, and fast-food restaurant employees rose in our society's estimation. We became aware that these workers were putting their lives on the line every day for us. And we were thankful for their selfless work. The pandemic showed us a new story about the meaning of work.

One of the Reformation's biggest contributions to Western culture was understanding the dignity of work within God's larger story.

What is the Triune God doing? What's my role in the larger, divine story of God's activities in the world? Within this scriptural narrative, "vocation" frames work as a divine call to serve the neighbor in response to God's grace in Christ. As we live in various communities, vocation defines how we participate in God's plan to build a new kingdom. These teachings were effectively summarized with the phrase *the priesthood of all believers.* This "priesthood" was a key understanding of the Reformation. The reality of this priesthood within the bigger story of God's kingdom connects Sunday and Monday on the calendar. Without this connection, the power of eighth-day discipleship is diminished.

The priesthood of all believers came to be used as a rubric to consolidate all the evangelical teachings about work. It was both a novel idea at the time and an ancient one, foreseen in Scripture as the apex of God's plan for humanity. "Worker-priests" scattered among "the nations" was the vision given to the children of Israel at Sinai (Exod 19:6) and through the prophet Isaiah (61:6). New Testament witnesses to this vision are found in Ephesians 3:12; 1 Peter 2:9; Hebrews 10:19–22; and Revelation 1:6. As Isaiah proclaims, "But you shall be called priests of the Lord, you shall be named ministers of our God" (Isa 61:6). As a worker-priest, life takes on a sacramental quality. Daily activities become sacrifices offered to God and directed toward the neighbor. Serving the neighbor becomes a form of worship. These are sacrifices of service offered in all our experiences—as parents, employees, neighbors, citizens, and church members. These priestly sacrifices please God because of Christ. Everyone gets to wear a clerical collar to work!

Concerning this daily sacrifice to serve the neighbor in the local and global economy, Gene Veith writes, "So the economic order, in light of the doctrine of vocation, becomes a complex network of individual human beings loving and serving each other according to their God-given abilities. The division of labor is transfigured into a labor of love."[15]

EIGHT-SIDED CHURCHES

So how does your work fit into God's bigger story? Remember the opening story I told about my encounter with the eight-sided church in Philippi (p. 1)? I couldn't understand the significance of eight-sided churches until our guide told us about the conviction of many early Christians that the day after Sunday (the day of resurrection) was not the first day of the week but rather the eighth day of creation. God's creative activity continued on this eighth day in the new and transformed life we experience in the risen Christ. The eighth day of creation is a day of resurrection work!

These early Byzantine Christians from Philippi knew the generative nature of the first day of the week for creating a new heaven and new earth. Resurrection was, finally, about not escaping but committing to the world that God so loved. These Philippians were at the starting blocks of a massive divine building project. God's rebuilding plan had begun (1 Cor 9:17). The New Testament was a witness to it. Jesus was the first fruit confirming it. Now they could experience "new creation" with their eyes, especially after the emperor Constantine converted to Christianity. The eight-sided basilica is a powerful testimony to how they viewed God working in their city and around the world.

The emphasis on "new creation" was contrasted to "the old" or "first creation." *The eighth day* is a term both intriguing and theologically rich. With their architecture as witness, these early Christians were proclaiming the gospel in a way that forced me to rethink the salvation story. God created the world in six days. On the seventh day, God rested. OK. This is where I had usually stopped telling the salvation story—that is, with God inviting us into God's shalom, God's salvation, God's rest. Heaven. I had no imagination for a call into another day of work, an eighth day.

In contrast, these fourth-century Christians from Philippi apparently understood that resurrection was not the end of the salvation story. Resurrection was not God's eternal retirement plan for the faithful. The eighth day was the beginning of an amazing architectural project focused on rebuilding the world. The resurrected Jesus was the first fruit of this exciting story. The church, as the body of Christ, was the second. The focus was on regeneration and renewal, not just the restoration of some glorious past (read "Eden"). The gospel message of resurrection was so intense that these Christians built their churches with eight sides to remember the call to resurrection work. Worshipping in an eight-sided church was like being surrounded and embraced by the gospel promise that God was creating something new. A new community. A new humanity. A new heaven and a new earth. A New Jerusalem. By worshipping in an eight-sided church, they chose to be shaped by Christ's call to eighth-day work. Redemption. Renewal. Regeneration. New, new, new!

THE IMPORTANCE OF THE NUMBER EIGHT

The number eight has a distinguished history in the Bible and in Jewish and Christian traditions.[16] The number was important to Jews and early Christians because of its rich symbolism. Eight members of Noah's family were saved in the time of the flood (Gen 7:13). First Peter then connects this story with baptism: "The ark . . . wherein a few, that is, eight souls, were saved by water. Whereunto baptism being of the like form, now saveth you also: not the putting away of the filth of the flesh, but the examination of a good conscience towards God by the resurrection of Jesus Christ" (1 Pet 3:20–21 DRA).

The royal house of Israel was built by King David, the eighth son of Jesse. It was on the eighth day of his life that a Jewish male child was circumcised. After the seven weeks of the spring harvest, in the Jewish calendar, the eighth day of the seventh week is Pentecost. In this same tradition, after the seventh day of the Feast of Tabernacles, there is an eighth day called the Last Great Day.

For Christians, the eighth- and fiftieth-day combination points to the final day of resurrection when the saints will be raised from the dead (1 Cor 15:2–13; John 3:3–12; Rev 20:4–6). The number eight symbolizes both circumcision of the heart for early Christians and the receiving of the Holy Spirit (Rom 2:28–29; Col 2:11–13). Finally, the number eight came to symbolize salvation in the Bible, as well as rebirth, regeneration, and new creation. It means being "born-again" or "born from above" (John 3:3).

Augustine is just one among many of the early church voices that picked up on this powerful symbol of resurrection: "The Sabbath, is the seventh day, but the Lord's day, coming after the seventh, must be the eighth, and is also to be reckoned the first." He writes, "The Day of the Lord is an everlasting eighth day." And again, "On the 8th day, God said, 'let the Church begin,' and it began."[17]

Eight-sided churches recall and testify to this resurrection story, reminding us of the first day of this new work by God, which will be completed when Jesus returns (the consummation). Whereas the seventh day represents rest, restoration, shalom, redemption, completion, and celebration, the eighth day represents work! New creation work. As far as the creation story goes, then, after a day of rest, God calls to us, "Follow me. Back to work!" Paul preaches in 2 Corinthians that "if anyone is in Christ, there is a new creation" (5:17). In other words, whoever is in Christ lives on the eighth day of creation and wears eighth-day lenses for viewing the world.

The implication of this message was astounding for me already back in 2012 in Philippi. The Sabbath rest wasn't the end of the Jesus story of salvation. Neither was I to skip too quickly to the final consummation. Rather, resurrection begins the architectural process of creating new (Rev 21). The resurrected Jesus is alive, sitting on the throne of God, and busy at work. From the throne of grace, Jesus calls his disciples to enter his divine work through the Spirit.

EIGHT-SIDED STORIES

In a fascinating move, Saint Ambrose (ca. 340–97) extends the lesson of church architecture to the design of baptismal fonts. He explains that a baptismal font is octagonal in shape "because on the eighth day, by rising, Christ loosens the bondage of death and receives the dead from their graves."[18] Many older churches still have their eight-sided baptismal fonts at the front or back of the sanctuary to tell this bigger story of God's redemptive activity beginning at baptism. When we are born again, we enter God's story of the eighth day of creation.

What is surprising, almost shocking, is that the work of Christ isn't to go back and restore the garden of Eden. The New Testament story acknowledges that the cherubim with swords of fire still guard the east entrance to the garden, thus protecting the tree of life. You can't go back, despite the message of Joni Mitchell's great song written in response to Woodstock: "We've got to get ourselves back to the garden." No, according to the biblical witness, we are called to move forward to a new city.

This eight-sided continuation of the creation story is therefore a break from the ancient tradition of epic storytelling where the hero leaves home, experiences an adventure, and then returns home enlightened. The *Odyssey* is an example of this epic story tradition. Odysseus leaves the island of Ithaca to fight at Troy. His return home to Penelope becomes an adventure. Enlightenment ensues as he finally returns to his native soil.

Americans have experienced this same epic story tradition through the classic movie *The Wizard of Oz*. Dorothy leaves Kansas, travels to Oz, and returns to Kansas enlightened. She concludes her adventure with the insight, "There's no place like home." The circle is complete: leave home, undergo an adventure, return home, experience enlightenment.

The biblical narrative flows differently. The story from Genesis to Revelation is linear, not circular. The story begins in a garden and ends in a city, moving forward to God's new design for life in New Jerusalem. This forward trajectory is essential for understanding the meaning of our daily work. The salvation story doesn't encourage us to return to the garden of Eden, as spiritually tempting as that may be. It points forward to a new life lived in freedom and responsibility within a new humanity. The point here is subtle but critical for our work. Eight-sided churches don't argue about what "life was like in the garden" or about the original "orders of creation." These churches don't fixate solely on rest from work either. Their focus is God's future. But let's not get too ahead of the story. First, a personal confession is in order.

A CONFESSION

Given the central meaning of God's big eighth-day salvation story discovered within the architecture of some ancient churches, I must make a confession. It's an awkward one. I should have known better, since I'm theologically trained and a church "insider." I served as a youth leader in Dayton, Ohio, and as a missionary in Germany and Zaire. I earned my PhD in theology and served as a professor of mission at two Lutheran seminaries and one Lutheran college. Furthermore, I was the director of a graduate program, an academic dean, and the president of a large Lutheran seminary. Finally, I worked for years as a consultant for theological schools all over the United States and Canada, supported by a Lilly Endowment and the Kern Family Foundation. Despite all my experience and training as a church insider, this big dimension of the gospel story eluded me. I overlooked the eighth day of creation. Or did I avoid it? Or was I trained to avoid it? I'm not sure, even today.

As a church insider, my ignorance in overlooking the "new creation" didn't trouble me. I've discovered only recently that this safe, status quo posture isn't sustainable. It's not actually safe; it's like living in a vulnerable house in Houston before a storm. More importantly, it's dangerous to the people I've been called to serve. My ignorance about God's "new creation" was particularly dangerous for the world that God so loves. By avoiding the eighth-day tradition, in essence . . . I lived comfortably in God's rest on Sundays. I avoided God's resurrection work on Mondays.

This confession about days of the week sounds trivial at first, and possibly puzzling. What does the calendar have to do with the meaning of the gospel story and my work? I started to discover in 2012 that the reality of this Sunday-Monday tension went to the heart of the church's core mission. If church leaders can't help their people connect Sunday to their daily lives, then what good are those "good shepherds"?

This insight bothered me from that moment in Philippi when I first encountered that eight-sided church structure. Congregational ministries are meant to lead people out into the world as disciples of Jesus. Discipleship for the life of the world is our goal—serving the world that God so loves. If a Christian leader can't shepherd a flock on how discipleship works in the real world from the perspective of the eighth day, then the rituals and language on Sunday become increasingly irrelevant. Sunday becomes reduced to one spiritual day isolated from the bigger story of God's new creation in Christ. The eighth day is avoided.

That was the crux of my problem. Sunday and Monday, and the separate worlds they represented, had become divided and divorced: "You are the salt of the earth; but if salt has lost its taste, how can its saltiness be restored? It is no longer good for anything, but is thrown out and trampled under foot" (Matt 5:13). Sunday was about spiritual performance, promoting people's piety and redemptive rites of personal growth at best, but not a witness to the bigger story of God's new creation in Christ. Even the practice of communion, where the story of God's cosmic redemption is told with beautiful clarity, was received merely by my people around the altar as personal atonement. That's all.

"Mondays" became centrally important during the Reformation. Regular work found meaning. The importance of work as a spiritual lifestyle overcame the monastic lifestyle as the true standard of obedience to Christ's commands, which emerged from the teaching on "justification by faith." Since Jesus had made us right with God through his death and resurrection, now our everyday lives could be focused on serving the neighbor in God's new order. Work became worship. Worship became service. The everyday work of the parent, nurse, farmer, carpenter, lawyer, soldier, and prince became spiritual. "Monday's work" became a high calling. Workers were priests.

Unfortunately, the culture of clericalism has often trumped the doctrine of "the priesthood of all believers" in most Lutheran congregations today. I can only speak about my own church tradition at this point. The eighth-day tradition of work as a divine call within God's larger story of redemption has been largely forgotten. A ministry focused on personal piety has won the day. Culture trumps doctrine. American culture, as we all know, elevates the individual.

The result is that our present culture of personal piety as Lutherans, and its preferred tool for delivery—clericalism—has completely dislodged a central teaching of the Reformation. The "priesthood of all believers" as a congregational practice has been domesticated. Congregations aren't really designed to teach discipleship for Monday's activities. Discipleship, taught from the perspective of vocation, isn't on the front burner of congregational life. It just isn't. Few congregations have been structured to promote vocation or to even talk about work.[19] Work and faith have been kept in separate corners. God's bigger story has been replaced by the story of personal piety leading to heaven. Our grasp of God's mission has thus been diminished.

CONFIRMATION OF THE DIVORCE

The obvious evidence of this divorce between Sunday and Monday existed everywhere in my parishes. A nasty divorce is hard to hide. To test the reality of the Sunday-Monday split (i.e., the sacred-secular split), our pastoral staff conducted one hundred interviews within our Lutheran congregation in Naples, Florida, asking the simple question: "How do you connect your faith with your daily life?" We used the excellent book by David Miller *God at Work*[20] to guide our questions. In the book, and based on his research, Miller maps out a matrix of four possible answers to the connection between faith and life. These "bridges" are the following:

- Evangelism: Work is a place for me to witness to my faith in Jesus Christ either directly with words or indirectly through my actions.
- Ethics: Work is a place where I live out my faith through strong moral commitments and values.
- Enrichment: Work is a place where I live out the knowledge, skills, and abilities God has given me. God has "wired" me a certain way through creation. I find fulfillment in work when I can use these gifts.

- Experience: Work is a place where I live out my vocational life. God has given me multiple calls, and work is the place where these "calls" are answered.

Our staff explored these dimensions of faith and life with our people on visits, ideally in the places where they worked. The location of the visit was crucial. By visiting our people at their places of employment, they could answer the questions from a position of strength. At church, the pastor knows all the "right answers." At work, in contrast, our people knew their own "world" better than anyone. Pastors were fish out of water.

The results of the survey brought both good and bad news and a few surprises. The good news was that many of our people did connect Sunday with Monday. The conversations were rich with testimonies about God's faithfulness in their work lives. All four of Miller's *e*'s were used to make the connection, albeit with evangelism being the one category cited most infrequently. Many started making these links already as young people. Others in college. Still others began making the connection between their faith and work recently, as adults. Each story was nuanced and personal, compelling and unique.

The bad news was twofold. First, no one placed their work within God's larger redemptive story of what God was doing in the world. Connecting faith and work was about them, not the world. Second, almost no one learned how to make this connection between faith and their daily lives in church. Wow! This was humbling to hear. Almost to a person, our people learned to connect faith and their daily work through influential people in their personal lives. Family, friends, parents, and mentors had the biggest impact; not sermons, worship services, Bible studies, catechesis, or pastoral visits. Consequently, very few could point to Bible passages that could help them bridge the gap between Sunday and Monday. The Bible inspired them, guided them, and equipped them "spiritually." But their work itself wasn't "spiritual." They had not learned the importance of work through any biblical and/or catechetical instruction.

Like a massive gong in a small room, the devastating assessment of clergy influence on connecting Sunday to Monday rang out. Almost to a person, our people didn't see their pastors as being of any assistance in making this vital connection. One person expressed this sentiment quite frankly: "It never would have occurred to me to ask my pastor about connecting faith to my work. I'm pretty sure our pastors wouldn't know how to do this [*making a wide gesture pointing around the office*]. It's not what I expect from them really."

Bill Diehl, a former leader of the Coalition for Ministry in Daily Life, relays this same message, albeit with more bite. His words remain a devastating critique of ministry that doesn't account for the eighth day:

> In the almost 30 years of my professional career, my church has never once suggested that there be any type of accounting of my on-the-job ministry to others. My church has never offered to improve those skills which could make me a better minister, nor has it ever asked if I needed any kind of support in what I was doing. There has never been an inquiry into the type of ethical decisions I must face, or whether I seek to communicate the faith to my coworkers. I have never been in a congregation where there was any type of public affirmation of a ministry in my career [as a sales manager for Bethlehem Steel]. In short, I must conclude that my church really doesn't have the least interest in whether and how I minister in my daily life.[21]

When you don't have an eighth day of creation story, and you don't claim to be an eight-sided church, then people's vocations and daily work don't really matter. God's mission is limited to the church and *its* Sabbath-day ministry.

Since 2012, my quest has been to help people make the connection between Sunday and Monday. I see a new call to mission within this architectural vision. I find inspiration in the call to be an eight-sided church, to live as an eight-sided Christian. I find a challenge in this expanded vision of mission. OK, how do I get there from here? First, take out your theological calendars.

THE SABBATH AND THE LORD'S DAY

Another day of the week starts now to become the major focus of the redemptive story. The eighth-day tradition enhances the Sabbath tradition. What does this mean? Jesus Christ's death and resurrection are God's answer to this dilemma of creation and fall. This resurrection life comes in two ways, represented symbolically by two days of the week, each playing a role within the story of redemption: the Sabbath and the Lord's Day. How do we understand and distinguish these two days?

> *Sabbath (Day 7 = Rest):* Jesus's death and resurrection restore our relationship with God and the world. Our sin is forgiven. We are redeemed. Shalom is established. We enter God's eternal rest. The mission on Day 7 is the care and redemption of the old order.

> *Lord's Day (Day 8 = Work):* Jesus's death and resurrection are a call into God's bigger plan of salvation for the world. This day represents an answer to the question, "What was our redemption for?" Answer: It was for the life of the world! Through Christ, God is creating a new heaven and earth through the power of this resurrected Jesus and his Spirit. The call to mission here is to enter God's eternal day of work because our salvation is secured by Jesus Christ.

To summarize, the Sabbath is a day when we celebrate a new relationship with God. It represents healing and finding that which had been lost. This day symbolizes the possibility of being freed from sin, death, and the devil. Day 7 represents the Year of Jubilee. It is a day when justice is restored. On Day 7, we find rest in Jesus.

The Lord's Day, the eighth day, on the other hand, is a day of work, when God calls us into the Triune God's plan of creating a new heaven and a new earth. It's about creating flourishing neighbors and neighborhoods. Not only does this day care for and preserve the old, but it also creates something new. Day 8 builds on the qualities of Day 7 ministries—preservation and restoration—and starts the work of new life and regeneration. It thrives with faith and freedom while envisioning God's power bursting forth from the grave into new forms of life.

The gospel story of redemption in Jesus Christ contains both resurrection messages, restoration and new creation. Eighth-day discipleship includes both the messages of the Sabbath (rest) and the Lord's Day (work).

WORK IN HEAVEN: WHAT'S THE STORY?

Now we have four ideas to wrestle with: the Sabbath, the Lord's Day, Sunday, and Monday. Are you confused yet? To make this day-of-the-week conflict simpler, answer one question: Is Sunday a day of rest or a day of work? Which is it for you? This is always a tough question for clergy. The clergy are known to sweat on Sundays. *Sweat* means "work." But what does this same question mean for people in the pews? One can test this tension by asking Christians a second question. Ask them about their vision of heaven. The answer will speak volumes about their imagination regarding the Sabbath (rest) or the Lord's Day (work).

Will there be work in heaven? Those steeped in the Lord's Day, the eighth-day tradition, will answer with an emphatic yes. They might even confess that for them the "heavenly" work has already begun. Eternal life comes with robes that double as overalls!

Those who have heard and embraced the Sabbath's gospel of "rest," in contrast, will answer no. Heaven frees us from work eternally. RIP. Heaven is for praise, fellowship, and worship, not work. It's an eternal Sunday morning at church complete with music, choirs, glorious praise, and great food around a catered banquet feast. Heaven is God's eternal, beatific retirement community.

How do you answer the work-in-heaven question? Do you embrace the day of rest (the Sabbath) or the day of work (the Lord's Day)? For much of my past ministry, I didn't speak about work or the theology behind these various days of the week. I left the teaching about work and vocation to the other church traditions less anxious about "work righteousness" and/or eschatological visions of the end times.[22] Nothing scares a Lutheran more than work righteousness. That is, nothing aside from the book of Revelation. We preach and teach that "all is a gift." Grace abounds. Sometimes that has left us ardently striving for spiritual passivity. It sounds funny, but Lutherans have a difficult time talking about work—and thus money and economics. This "fear" betrays our strong theological tradition of vocation through service. This deficiency is linked with how we read both the creation story and the book of Revelation. Gaps exist in our gospel story.

Similarly, while other Protestant traditions spend time on pre- or postmillennial debates,[23] Lutherans mostly just avoid altogether any sort of prediction regarding the "end times." Heaven is for us about our life with God behind those pearly gates, not about some larger story unfolding in the world. As a result of this shrinkage of the grand biblical narrative, we have tragically lost much of the big picture of God's mission that is painted by the New Testament. This big story, in my own preaching, had been "left behind." Our church's mission was simple: to serve the neighbor on the way to heaven. Service to the neighbor, of course, doesn't help us gain God's favor, but it isn't part of any bigger picture of God's redemptive purpose for the world either. Serving the neighbor gives us Lutherans something to do on the grace-filled road to heaven. Heavenly rest is the goal: Eternal retirement without worries, pain, or tears. Roads paved with gold. A mansion within a gated community. Lots of praise. Good choral music. Bach on the organ. So the message of "heavenly rest" has dominated Sunday morning, our preaching, the practice of communion, and our funerals.

As I started reading my tradition's sixteenth-century texts, I found that in sharp contrast, the talk about work as vocation "in the last days" consumed Martin Luther. He believed that if you didn't understand work (e.g., vocation), you hadn't understood the gospel. The whole *Small Catechism* talks about the call into our vocations as a priestly call. Vocation involves sweat. Even suffering and sacrifices. Our work matters to God. How had I lost this fundamental dimension of my religious tradition? How could I get it back?

CONCLUSION

Encountering the national conversation around "faith, work, and economics" has given me fresh lenses to go back and discover anew the fullness of my Reformation tradition as presenting an architecture for discipleship. Entering this movement has allowed me to engage the challenge I first encountered at the eight-sided basilica in Philippi in 2012. What might I learn from these early Christians about the meaning of faith and daily work? Later, Martin Luther wrote his whole catechism to teach his people about work and vocation as the centerpieces of discipleship. I wondered, "As Luther discussed work, did he also engage with economic debates in his catechism?" The next chapter addresses that question. As we shall see, nothing clarifies our daily work more than living in the story of the eighth day.

In modern Israel beneath the ancient Megiddo prison, an archaeological excavation has revealed the headquarters of two Roman legions that occupied the biblical areas of Judea and Samaria.[24] Excavators have discovered a room that functioned as one of the earliest Christian churches we've found in the Holy Land. Archaeologists date the site to circa 230 CE—that is, one of very few Christian churches that dates to a period before the Edict of Milan in 313 CE, when the Roman Empire officially recognized Christianity and protected it. Why is this worship site so important? It served as an early place of Christian worship for Roman soldiers, and it was built with an octagonal shape.

For gentile Christians, like these Roman officers, eight was the number that symbolized resurrection. Just as the old creation began on the first day of the week, so now the new creation would begin on the Lord's Day, the eighth day. It is for this reason that many Christian churches built during the Byzantine period—and ever since—are eight-sided structures.

The Roman Catholic catechism today lifts up the importance of the number eight within this same framework: "The eighth day. But for us a new day has dawned: the day of Christ's Resurrection. The seventh day completes the first creation. The eighth day begins with the new creation. Thus, the work of creation culminates in the greater work of redemption. The first creation finds its meaning and its summit in the new creation in Christ, the splendor of which surpasses that of the first creation."[25]

Embracing the eighth day of creation changes our approach and understanding of work. Nevertheless, what does eighth-day work mean practically? What is the architecture, so to speak, of an eight-sided church? And what might it mean to live and work as an eight-sided Christian?

My project here is a simple one: I want to return to the Reformation tradition to uncover any answers to these work-related questions. Does the eighth-day story exist within my religious tradition, connecting Sunday and Monday? Have our foreparents in the faith been inviting us into this conversation all along? Have they left us eighth-day bread crumbs along the path?

I turn to these questions next.

3

Eighth-Day Christians

Living in God's Home Economics Project

> Today the whole relation of the Christian church to the
> secular realm stands front and center on the stage. . . .
> The disciple is challenged to help and befriend [their]
> neighbor in every bodily need, and to do this in the name
> of Christ. That function can scarcely be served without in
> some way helping [them] to improve [their] livelihood . . .
> and find their own indigenous economic basis.
> —William Danker, *Profit for the Lord*

To be faithful and effective, workers must understand the overall purpose of their organization.[1] Many companies, schools, and nonprofits
discuss the mission, vision, and values of their organizations before
hiring any worker. Why? The big picture motivates and clarifies!
Leaders want to know if their workers, from top to bottom, fit into
the larger picture of the organization's mission.

The purpose of economics, in this context, is to first paint the
big picture. Economics defines reality. As a Christian, this big vision
points to the story of God's management and stewardship of the
world. Grasping God's economics consequently clarifies the meaning
and purpose of one's daily work too.

Economics embraces stories big and small. God's economics
reflects the big picture of God's governance of the world while exploring the details of that management in every person's daily life. Is management working? Has stewardship been effective and efficient? Even
in the kingdom of God, as we shall see, numbers tell an important

story about whether our work is functioning justly, righteously, and according to God's will. God is always in the numbers.

Our focus, consequently, now shifts from the relationship between faith and work to the relationship between faith and economics. Watch now as the red warning signs start flashing. The relationship between faith and economics brings massive discomfort to religious leaders and theologians. In fact, in my experience, no topic will press a person's spirituality or challenge a congregation more within their neighborhood than the relationship between faith and economics. When you talk numbers, the story of God's mission is at stake.

TAKING A "HOME ECONOMICS" WALK

The importance of connecting faith and economics took root in my heart and mind right after returning from Turkey and Greece. A modest walk from my home to the campus of the University of Minnesota dramatically changed my whole imagination around discipleship as life within an eighth-day creation story. Whereas the trip to Turkey and Greece animated an internal conversation concerning the connection between faith and *work*, this walk focused my attention on deepening the relationship between faith and *economics*.

My experience began early on a beautiful summer morning. As I walked across the Saint Paul campus, I stopped to admire an older building that had been meticulously renovated. You could see from the design that the building was from another era, although now refurbished. On the top of the building, the department's original name from the 1930s had been preserved. Engraved on the beam stretching across the brick structure was "Home Economics."

My relationship to the discipline of home economics at that point was meager. I remember a course by that name from my high school back in the 1970s. The boys in my high school would take "shop." The girls—and some of the football players, to increase their grade point average—would take "home ec." Naturally, as a high school student, I had no idea of the background of these classes within the curriculum.

The formal field of home economics in the United States dates to the mid-nineteenth century, though the idea of "economics" itself goes all the way back to Greek philosophers and their ideas surrounding "household management."[2] That history became the foundation for this international educational movement, especially among women.

Home economics is a scientific and practical field of study that deals with the management of the home, family, and community.[3] Classes on the subject remained popular in colleges and high schools up until the 1960s. The early proponents of home economics were leaders who wished to bring science to bear on the practical skills of running the home. The goal was to improve the quality of life for families and communities and especially to educate rural farm wives about how best to run their households within various local environments. An act of Congress in 1862 encouraged these courses to be taught in a few Midwestern land-grant colleges, like those in Minnesota. Classes were first offered in the United States, but they quickly spread to other countries. These classes were promoted to assist a nation in building a larger economy on the strength of the family home.

How did the terminology surrounding home economics take shape? Late in the nineteenth century, a study group was organized to discuss the essence of the domestic sciences. They met in Lake Placid, New York. Various names for the emerging discipline were suggested and rejected: for example, *oekology*, or the science of right living, and *eudaimonia*, or the science of "happiness." *Euthenics*, the science of controllable environment, was also considered. *Home economics* was ultimately chosen because of its long history and broad application around topics such as management, stewardship, finance, budgeting, food, cooking, kitchen and home appliances, pedagogy, childcare, clothing, and environmental topics. The American Home Economics Association was founded in 1909.

Home economics departments within colleges spread rapidly and offered a curriculum that included studies in nutrition, the preparation of food, flourishing gardens, interior design, clothing and textiles, child health and development, family relationships, and yes, household finances. As a result, *economics* was the term used to describe the big picture of how a home might thrive and flourish within a given context.

THE ECONOMIC MIRACLE OF 2012

Then came my own economic miracle during that same summer. I had come to embrace this wonderful word *economics* because of the way it described household management and stewardship. I also appreciated how the history of the word went back to the Greeks. Being a Christian, however, I wanted to employ a more biblical, theological word for this same concept.

Then came the discovery. As I explored and studied the New Testament, the word used in it to describe the dynamics and function of the Greek idea of economics ("home management") was—drum roll, please—*economics*. The same word! How could I have missed this important concept in my Bible training? Or was I ever really taught the vital connection between God's activity in the world and economics? I couldn't remember any mention of it at the seminary, with one striking exception: lectures on the Holy Trinity. The Triune God's activity in the world was described with the technical term the *economic trinity*. This "work" dimension of God was philosophically contrasted with the "being" of God. Act (work) and being (essence) were thus two theological dimensions for understanding the divine reality.

Have you lost interest in this discussion yet? If so, that points to the problem. Talk about the economic trinity seems abstract and unrelated to daily living. Some Christians use the language of "God's mission" to describe the same divine reality. Unfortunately, during those early years in seminary, I didn't make the practical connection of God's activities bridging Sunday and Monday that the early church's trinitarian theologians were trying to make. The idea went over my head. I never used the term *economics* in my ministry.

Furthermore, I didn't evaluate economic language as important for congregational ministry because nobody else seemed to do so either. At least, that is, no congregational leader I knew. I should note that I obviously wasn't regularly attending any Black churches, where preachers often spoke on such matters. I also wasn't making the right connections between my ministry and the speeches of Martin Luther King Jr., where phrases such as *justice for the poor, social engagement*, and *loving the neighbor* are used frequently. So the link between a larger notion of economics and mission just didn't happen. When I thought about the poor, the word *charity* came to mind, not direct economic activity. Around the spiritual kitchen table, so to speak, no one was talking about economics.

I came to realize that a negative notion of economics had shaped me in profound ways. My spirituality needed, I believed, to be guarded from the world. "Money talk" just wasn't proper or spiritual. Wasn't the love of money, after all, the root of all evil? This was certainly a misguided bias, I now admit. This position also reflected a poor and inaccurate use of Scripture (1 Tim 6:10). But it did define much of our church's culture around money and business. Many Christians still believe that money compromises true spirituality. So too does business. The idea is that true discipleship must avoid the inevitable stain of economic activity. Money is bad for your soul. God is certainly not to be found in the dog-eat-dog dynamic of the capitalist marketplace.[4]

If you accept this negative worldview about economics, Mondays seem to be a dangerous day for sanctification. I realize now that my attitudes reflected a certain tradition of pre-Reformation monastic Christianity. Spirituality could only prosper apart from the world, not in it. I thought that the walls of the church, like the monastery walls centuries ago, were there to protect my faith.

This brand of monastic spirituality ironically was challenged by the Reformation. At the core of the evangelical (Protestant) movement of the sixteenth century was the experience of grace in daily life. This "experience" wasn't an abstract idea. Grace was "earthy" and real. The experience involved regular people being in the presence of a gracious God through Christ by faith. Martin Luther's life reflected the concreteness of this transformation. After 1517, Luther was given the monastery where he had lived the vows of chastity, obedience, and poverty as a monk, and he made that same building into his new home, which soon included a wife, kids, a brewery, and all his other "worldly" interests. In other words, Luther's old monastic home was thoroughly transformed to become his new home, where he lived a completely different existence within the community. Same building, different lifestyle. Different lifestyle, different economy. After all, Luther—with his wife, Katie—had to feed all of the children who gathered around the kitchen table each day.

Consequently, the Reformation defined the big story of divine activity in the world as the Triune God's home economics project! Furthermore, the bulk of this work centered on engaging regular people outside the walls of their church buildings. The laity in this home economics project were to serve as the chief channels of God's management of the world and community in Christ.

Please note: This insight about the importance of laity in God's economy isn't about disparaging clergy. It's just a matter of grasping the divine organizational chart. The people of God have been called to do a lot of work all week long! Good work. God's work. God's home economics plan is to call all people to work in God's household. More specifically, God's desire is to govern the world through their work. That's God's economy!

The central point is that God works through people every day to carry out God's will and reign over all things. The divine economy has a workforce, an organizational chart, and an action plan. The eighth-day creation story now takes on a new character. The laity are now key players in God's economy. "The laity" here means the scattered Monday people of God, not simply the gathered community on Sunday.

As the notion of economics as a way to describe God's big story—the eighth day—took shape in my imagination, I found I still needed a few more puzzle pieces to make sense of the emerging picture. So I turned to the Bible.

THE BIBLE AND ECONOMICS

Let's explore the Bible for ideas about economics. The first biblical insight links the confession "Jesus is Lord" and the Greek term for "economics." Older church traditions grasped these insights right from the beginning. Unfortunately, this link has been largely lost.

Within the liturgical calendar, for example, the celebration of one of the great festivals of the church, the Feast of the Ascension, is a celebration of Jesus's enthronement in heaven. The word "great" here is used with some hesitation. Many Christians who follow liturgical traditions might not remember when and how this day is celebrated each year. In nonliturgical traditions, the festival isn't celebrated at all, of course, but the story is told because biblical references to Jesus's ascension are found throughout the New Testament (Mark 16:19; Luke 24:51; John 14:2; Acts 1:10–11; Rom 8:34; Eph 1:20–21; Heb 10:12; 1 Pet 3:22). But why are these texts so critical to the whole story of Jesus?

On old liturgical calendars, Ascension Day is celebrated between Easter and Pentecost. The pivotal story is not just about Jesus disappearing into the clouds with the disciples below gazing into the sky. The key to the festivities is that Jesus has taken his place on the throne of God, sitting next to the Father. Jesus is now ruling the world from the throne of God! This is the initial meaning of God's economics: namely, Jesus is Lord! As Abraham Kuyper famously said, "There is not a square inch in the whole domain of our human existence over which Christ, who is Sovereign over all, does not cry, Mine!"[5]

Everything is under King Jesus's rule. That is the first basic tenet of Christian economics.

This fundamental economic reality is boldly asserted when Christians confess the Apostles' Creed: that Jesus "ascended into heaven [and] is seated at the right hand of the Father." What is Jesus doing on that throne, sitting at the right hand of God? Jesus is governing the world, of course, managing and stewarding creation. Put bluntly, Jesus is Lord over this world, *not just my personal life*. Consequently, economics helps us elevate the complex reality of confessing that Jesus is Lord and that Jesus sits on a throne next to the Father, managing, stewarding, and governing the world. The ascension is essential for God's home economics plan. This throne room where he is "seated at the right hand of the Father" is a major dimension of the bigger story of the eighth day of creation.

The use of the term *economics* here is naturally referring to a wider range of topics than just finance. Economics encompasses every dimension of God's rule in Christ, not just dollars and cents. But it also includes the dollars and cents. This big economic story includes a swirl of human relationships lived out through a complex process of human interactions involving the exchange of goods and services, production and consumption, as well as creating and expressing value and relationships. Relationships and the value given to those relationships are at the core of any talk about economics.

Economics, therefore, involves an angle of vision that is both spiritually generative and theologically provocative. It looks at, studies, and evaluates all dimensions of life to see how things are working, should work, or will work. The Lordship of Jesus is deeply entwined with the whole concept of economics—that is, the management and stewardship of all things.

WHAT DOES SCRIPTURE SAY ABOUT ECONOMICS?

The connection between Jesus's Lordship and economics can be difficult to discover in the Bible because of the various English translations used for *oikonomia*, the Greek word for "economy." A review of *oikonomia* in the New Testament reveals its use nine times:

- Luke 16:2–4, three times (translated "management" or "stewardship")
- 1 Corinthians 9:17 (translated "stewardship," "administration," "commission," or "dispensation")
- Ephesians 1:10 (translated "administration" or "dispensation")
- Ephesians 3:2 (translated "stewardship," "dispensation," or "administration")

- Ephesians 3:9 (translated "administration")
- Colossians 1:25 (translated "stewardship," "dispensation," or "administration")
- 1 Timothy 1:4 (translated "administration" or "stewardship")[6]

Thus, several different words are consistently used to embrace the Greek notion of "economy." This makes sense, since the Greek word *oikonomia*, which could also be translated as "house management," was used by Greek philosophers to include all the major tasks of the home, family, and business. *Management, stewardship, administration, dispensation, arrangement, plan, commission,* and *governance* were all terms used to describe the work of a person, such as the steward or the servant in many biblical texts, assigned to look after another's affairs. "Economy" (*oikonomia*) brought all these concepts together neatly.

It is difficult to understand the central message of the Bible without economic images. They are everywhere! Jesus and the gospel come wrapped in the swaddling clothes of economic ideas. The focus on economics compels us to reconsider the nature of incarnation, redemption, and the eighth day of creation. It raises basic questions: How is God managing God's creation? What is God's plan for the world in Christ? How does God include us in God's stewardship of the earth? How have the affairs of our neighbor been left to our care? Concerning the Triune God's kingdom, how do we describe the present dispensation? What does the Year of Jubilee mean for us today? How does redemption work? How are both sins and debts forgiven? What gifts have we received personally and as a church to manage and administer our various vocations in this life? What are the economic implications of "love for neighbor?" The answers to these questions will help define God's economics in Christ.

CREATION AND CALL

Economics raises an important question about God's plan for us and the world: What is our salvation for?[7] To address this question we need to start at the beginning. In the creation stories in Genesis, we learn a lot about economics and work. In fact, the stories of creation in Genesis are also stories about call, vocation, and economics. From Genesis 1 and 2, we learn that humanity was created in the image of God and assigned at least five tasks or vocations in the garden. Humanity was

- to have "dominion" over creation (Gen 1:26),
- to be "fruitful and multiply, and fill the earth" (Gen 1:28),
- to "till" and "keep" creation (Gen 2:15),
- to "name" the animals (Gen 2:19), and
- to form marriages or partnerships (Gen 2:18).

In other words, our work from the beginning included

- the call to govern and create order in the world,
- the call to be productive and fruitful with all creation,
- the call to work in and guard creation,
- the call to name and discover creation's order, and
- the call to build families and fill the earth.

These five "calls" tied to God's creation richly describe the purpose and meaning of daily life. All the "garden calls" need to be mentioned together because they balance and complement one another. They also form an initial basis for approaching God's economy in the world. God's creation, God's call, and God's economy all find their initial impulses in Genesis.

There is much new literature that has rediscovered this old insight that celebrates the link between the garden with its economy and call.[8] God's economy started when God created the first "household" with Adam and Eve.[9] To be made in the image and likeness of God meant that humanity was endowed through God's call to accept responsibility for creation with God. The first household, therefore, was instructed to work together in the garden to till, maintain, and guard it.

The Greek word in the New Testament for "house" is *oikos*. You can see how this root word is related to *oikonomia*. *Economy* ("house management") and *ecumenical* ("all in one house") are rooted in these words. Theologians and Bible teachers bring this image of "household management" from the Genesis story into our present experience in creative ways.[10] The analogies have become numerous, especially concerning issues surrounding the environment. For example, Sallie McFague writes, "We need to learn how 'home economics' functions; that is, the basic rules of how our 'garden home' can prosper—and what will destroy it."[11]

Luther's "Priesthood of All Believers" takes up this same economic theme and ties it to the role of "vocation" in the everyday life of a Christian. The book of Revelation ends with the creation of a new city where the three *w*'s of the garden of Eden are reestablished: (1) walking with God, (2) working with God, and (3) worshiping God in the NEW Jerusalem. These three *w*'s summarize our vocational lives as priests. Eighth-day disciples and churches, therefore, make the connections among their faith, work, and the larger story of God's rule in Christ—that is, God's economy. Eighth-day discipleship integrates these same dynamics to connect Sunday with Monday.

ECONOMICS AND THE "THEREFORE" OF MISSION

How do the terms in all these economic references in the Bible function with one of the church's core mandates, "to preach the gospel to all nations"? At the heart of God's economic activity is evangelism. In fact, it's God's economic story about Jesus that gives this great commission its power and authority. The expression of this idea in the text of Matthew is all about the "therefore": "Now the eleven disciples went to Galilee, to the mountain to which Jesus had directed them. When they saw him, they worshiped him; but some doubted. And Jesus came and said to them, 'All authority in heaven and on earth has been given to me. *Go therefore* and make disciples of all nations, baptizing them in the name of the Father and of the Son and of the Holy Spirit, and teaching them to obey everything that I have commanded you. And remember, I am with you always, to the end of the age'" (Matt 28:16–20; emphasis mine). Almost all the books of the New

Testament have their own "great commission." The text in Matthew, however, has become a bedrock for the church's articulation of its mission. This commission summarizes Matthew's Gospel and calls us into the world as disciples of Jesus. As we read the text closely, we see that Jesus's mission mandate hangs on the story before the word *therefore*. As one of my earliest Bible teachers emphasized, "When you read a *therefore* in the Bible, ask what the *therefore* is *there for*." Jesus's commission to his disciples definitely depends on the content before the "therefore." The disciples are to go into all the world because "all authority in heaven and on earth has been given to me." Without Jesus's authority in heaven and on earth, there is no great commission and no mission.

God's economic activity in the world depends, therefore, on this bigger story of what has happened to Jesus of Nazareth. He has been raised and sits at the right hand of the Father. "Therefore . . . go." The whole task of evangelism implies the enthronement of the Son of God. Consequently, Jesus can only be my personal Lord and Savior because he has been given the Lordship of all creation. Jesus sits on the throne with power and authority. That's the bigger story.

In summary, the "economics of God" found in the New Testament describes God's bigger plan for the universe in Christ. It incorporates God's rule in Christ (the kingdom of God) and how Christ includes us in his reign (God's mission). God's plan is thus bigger than my personal redemption story. Economics here includes all the steward-ship and management numbers and must address the question, "For what?" God liberates us from sin, death, and the devil for a purpose. God grants us shalom for a bigger plan. Our work does not make sense without the bigger story of redemption.

The answer to "For what?" is the story about the eighth day of creation. Being attached to the Triune God brings us into alignment with God's activities in our neighborhood. God is creating a new heaven and earth. A new city. A new community. Our calling as chil-dren of God is to participate in this new creation work. It's God's work. Our mission.

THE GOSPEL STORY,
THE REFORMATION, AND ECONOMICS

The early church fathers understood the connection between mission and economics. So too did the Reformers. God's economy describes the character and trajectory of God's redemptive work in the world, which calls forth an eight-sided church filled with worker-priests.

Economics will always be tied to gospel proclamation. They are intrinsically linked. Because of the renewed experience of the gospel, for example, Luther's Germany began to prosper economically. Cities throughout Europe wanted to replicate the innovations from Wittenberg so that they might also grow. Why should anyone be surprised by this connection between faith and economic growth? Very often, however, we are. The economic side of the Reformation is a story rarely told, which diminishes the whole evangelical movement's impact.[12] It's this economic side of the story that needs to be rediscovered today.

By 1521, Luther had money to invest. Monastic piety—built on poverty, chastity, and obedience—had given way to a new evangelical spirituality lived out by regular people in their daily lives. Luther taught that the key to evangelical spirituality was living out of one's vocation in response to the gospel. So many monks and nuns had left the monasteries. That left Luther with a problem: What was to be done with all that abandoned church property? The monasteries were now empty. What should they do with these assets? The Reformers made a brilliant decision: sell the monasteries and invest the capital—in people! The teaching of vocation by evangelical churches, in other words, led to the realization that the church had to invest in its people and their vocations as worker-priests. This investment became a significant part of the church's mission strategy and, in turn, would grow both the church's mission and the city's economic capacity. Good numbers followed.[13]

Luther invested in people's vocations because he wanted to prepare them for their daily work in Wittenberg. Theological convictions guided these actions. Daily work, Luther taught, was their ministry from God. What made this decision remarkable was that Luther had other good options for investing the money. He could have considered military infrastructure, for example. The Turks were already in Vienna and threatening the Holy Roman Empire. Or he could have built larger, more glorious churches to compete with Roman congregations. Compare, as a useful exercise, Henry VIII's use of these same monies from church properties sold in Protestant England. The contrast is striking.

Luther had discovered the power of the eighth-day story of creation. The role of the laity as worker-priests emerged as critical to God's big story. As a result, the evangelicals in Wittenberg invested in their people and in their daily callings. Hospitals, libraries, public schools, and universities were built. And a community chest was created to increase the effectiveness of various local investments.[14] The church encouraged investment in its people and in their city because the laity were recognized as the true missionaries building the kingdom from Monday through Saturday.

Carter Lindberg writes about Luther at this time in the following way:

Although some scholars have described Luther as the first political economist, Luther understood himself as a pastor and theologian radicalized by the grasp of justification by grace alone. We are named in God's last will and testament, and since Christ, the testator, has died the will is in effect and we have inherited all that is Christ's. Since salvation is received—not achieved—salvation is the foundation for life not its goal. Hence both poverty and almsgiving lose saving significance. Justification by grace alone undercut the explanatory function of the medieval ideology of poverty that fatalistically presented poverty and riches as the divine plan. . . . Under the rubric of Deuteronomy 15:4, "There will be no poor among you," Luther and his Wittenberg colleagues proceeded to establish social welfare programs. Luther was concerned to develop prophylactic as well as remedial social assistance. "For so to help a man that he does not need to become a beggar is just as much of a good work and a virtue as to give alms to a man who has already become a beggar."[15]

How do we live the redemptive life on Monday as an eight-sided church? One answer is to have the church invest in its people and their calls as worker-priests. That's where faith in Christ will certainly take us. The church is thus turned inside out. Instead of just providing leadership training for our people to serve "the church" and its mission (read: the gathered church), the church now provides leadership training for its people to serve their neighbors through their daily activities at home, work, and school and in their neighborhoods. Send your people out as worker-priests! Equip everyone, so to speak, to wear their clerical collars to work on Monday.

COMPETING NARRATIVES

Unfortunately, we are surrounded by alternative stories that don't move us forward. There still are enemies of God's economy even today. These false narratives call out to us constantly like those siren songs tempting Odysseus to the rocks: "Whoever draws too close, off guard, and catches the sirens' voice in the air—no sailing home for him. . . . Race straight past that coast."[16] The point is that the call to live as an eight-sided church does not come to us within a vacuum. The counternarratives in our culture compete with the evangelical story told in Scripture and addressed in Luther's catechisms. What are those siren songs? In Luther's day, the competing worldviews came from the pope (sale of indulgences), Aristotle (ethics), Erasmus (reason), local princes (politics and money), Charles V (political unity), and Zwingli (the nature of grace). Whereas these narratives are still important to study and debate, some of the most pressing competing narratives today are different. They are a product of our American culture. We've heard their tunes and we know their verses. Although they sound sweet, these songs can lead travelers straight to the rocks.

Four counternarratives were briefly outlined in chapter 1. Now let me highlight these same worldviews in more detail. There are other competing stories, of course. I have chosen these four narratives because I've observed their allure in the congregations that I've served. They are tempting, and they have economic consequences. Christians respond to them daily. Some may even mistakenly consider them a part of the Christian songbook. These stories dominate our families, our places of employment, and our economic lives. Consequently, we consider these stories enemies of the evangelical story of God's eighth day of creation and economy.

An Economic Counterstory: *Homo Economicus*

The first counternarrative revolves around a particular definition of the human being that has emerged from modern economic theory, sometimes described by the Latin term *homo economicus*, which describes human beings as autonomous, rational, self-interested, material beings.[17]

It is one attempt to answer the question, What helps us thrive and prosper? "It [*homo economicus*] comes from the concept of a rational individual who, led by narrowly egotistical motives, sets out to maximize his benefit." This economic theory provides a guiding principle for living life based on self-interest. *Economics* is a "study of human relationships that are sometimes expressed in numbers, a study that deals with tradeables, but one that also deals with nontradeables."[18] The power and threat of *homo economicus* as a moral theory is that it attempts to define and govern everything.

With this definition of a human being, the theory predicts that we, along with our fellow neighbors, will act out of our own rational self-interest in all economic relationships.[19] God is not part of the equation. Neither are love, virtue, freedom, and sacrifice. Individual self-interest reigns in the market, this theory affirms. The theory even predicts that as people follow their own individual self-interests in a free market, the system works more efficiently in response to needs. An "invisible hand" transforms private self-interest into public good. Somehow it all works out. *Homo economicus* translates into an economic order that values transactions that are efficient and growth oriented, promoting self-interest and praising individualism and freedom.

Homo economicus is such a powerful theory of human behavior that it has grown to influence life outside of economics, including politics, education, health care, family planning, and many more dimensions of life. This economic theory has even reached into our religious lives. That shows just how important economic matters are to our culture. Economics influences how we understand ourselves, our families, our neighborhoods, our nations, our churches, and our God!

Since materialism and consumption play heroic roles within the dynamic of *homo economicus*, society inevitably becomes more materialistic and consumer oriented. Consumption is, after all, a supreme good in this worldview. Growth in consumption is of paramount importance. As this worldview stresses the priorities and possibilities of self-interest, society becomes focused inward. Another Latin term, *homo incurvatus in se*, refers to life turned inward toward oneself rather than outward toward the neighbor. Some might call this a definition of "sin." Certainly, a life turned inward and based on materialistic drivers is less sacrificial and, ultimately, greedy. Dog-eat-dog ethics can be justified in many business environments because "that's just how business works." Competition among churches takes on this same character. People go "church shopping." The best church wins! We often hear justifications of harsh actions in the business community like, "It wasn't meant to be personal; it's just business." This dynamic sometimes functions now among churches as well.

Americans have created a public economic marketplace—an economic cathedral—around the notion of *homo economicus*, and this financial and moral edifice, like any good architecture, is shaping our whole lives.

A Second Economic Counterstory: Prosperity Gospel

This second counterstory equates money and physical well-being with the fruits of faith. It is similar to *homo economicus*, except it does not view the person's desire for wealth as materialistic. Rather, people are spiritual and have a relationship to God. How does one build their relationship with God? By investing in the divine relationship. Be faithful in all things, and God will reward you with material blessings, healing, and prosperity. This story depends in part on the concept of *homo economicus* above and partially on well-selected texts from Scripture. Its power lies in gaining the power of divine approval. In this story, God wants to bless you with treasures from God's storehouse of grace. All you need to do is to show God your faith. Invest in your relationship with God. Your positive attitude, speech, and financial contributions will be the evidence of this faith-filled investment. These seeds of faith will grow and produce fruit, showering you with God's blessings. Since God wants you to thrive and prosper, your faith is the only thing standing between you and God's gift of prosperity. Exercise your faith and then watch the blessings flow. The prosperity gospel story is flourishing in America and around the world.

This economic story is as old as the pagan cults of Greece and Rome. The whole pagan sacrificial system was built on this same thinking. The faithful were to bring sacrifices to the gods to please them. But that's the rub: When do you know that God is truly pleased with your gifts? When it rains? When you are healed? When that hoped-for baby is born? When the crop is successful? When your "ship" comes in? When your armies are victorious? This counterstory, in the end, can dig a massive hole of insecurity deep within any believer. When is my sacrificial gift enough for God? The practice of indulgences in the Reformation era was promoted and practiced based on the same human impulses.

A Religious Counterstory: Moralistic Therapeutic Deism

A third counternarrative to the biblical story is referred to by Christian Smith in his excellent study of young people's spirituality, *Soul Searching*,[20] as moralistic therapeutic deism (MTD). In his observations of the spirituality of teenagers, Christian Smith outlined the following five tenets of MTD:

- A God exists who creates, orders, and watches over the world.
- God wants people to be moral, good, and fair.
- The central goal of life is to be happy and to feel good about oneself.
- God is not involved in one's life except to solve problems.
- Good people go to heaven when they die.[21]

When the researchers evaluated young people, it was clear that these theological understandings were alive and well in their lives. Interestingly, Smith concluded that young people learned these "articles of faith" from their parents. How unfortunate! This insight resonates with my own congregational experience. Unless a person has had strong Christian teaching, they easily fall prey to this MTD story. The seductive story line is that life's goals are to be happy and healthy and to go to heaven. God isn't really needed or present in our daily lives unless something bad happens. That's when we pray.

Many self-professed Christians read the five MTD tenets and nod approvingly, affirming them as sound doctrine. They might embrace this belief system or at least compare it favorably over against the belief system of a "secular" person or an "atheist." After all, its adherents believe in God, heaven, and strong moral teaching. It's humbling to discover or admit as a pastor that after all the sermons and Bible studies, many people can't tell the difference between the biblical story of faith in the Triune God and a whimsical form of deism. This counterstory must be called out for what it is: a flimsy architectural design upon which to build your life.

A Cultural Counterstory: Triumphant Tribalism

Tribalism comes naturally to all people. It creates ties that bind, including economic ties. Tribalism is constructive when it knows its place and limits. Its power to build community is simply a part of God's created order. Like all of creation, it is good. It's a gift. Praise God. In community, we are loyal to our families, our cultural and religious groups, and the nations in which we are raised and that formed us as human beings. This loyalty, again, is natural and can be pleasing to God. Culture, language, religious rituals, laws, music, literature, civic pride, and more bind us together and emerge from our lives in community.

The gospel reminds us that, despite these beautiful aspects of the created order, our ultimate loyalty must remain to God. No triumphalism may be attached to any specific community. The Bible calls this jumbling of priorities "idolatry." Idolatry is misdirected love. As idolatry, triumphant tribalism becomes a counternarrative to the gospel. Because the love of a tribe (e.g., family, community, church, ethnicity, nation, etc.) is such a powerful force in our lives, the first commandment addresses this temptation right up front: "You shall have no other gods." "Other gods" here means anything in which we place our ultimate love and trust aside from God. This can mean money and property, power and influence, family and friends, nation and culture, and even church and denomination. These are all good things, but they mustn't replace God as God.

When Jesus speaks to this matter, his words are so jarring that we must often read his admonitions twice or three times:

And he [Jesus] was told, "Your mother and your brothers are standing outside, wanting to see you." But he said to them, "My mother and my brothers are those who hear the word of God and do it." (Luke 8:20–21)

I came to bring fire to the earth, and how I wish it were already kindled! . . . Do you think that I have come to bring peace to the earth? No, I tell you, but rather division! From now on five in one household will be divided, three against two and two against three; they will be divided: father against son and son against father, mother against daughter and daughter against mother, mother-in-law against her daughter-in-law and daughter-in-law against mother-in-law. (Luke 12:49–53)

Whoever comes to me and does not hate father and mother, wife and children, brothers and sisters, yes, and even life itself, cannot be my disciple. (Luke 14:26)

But when he saw many Pharisees and Sadducees coming for baptism, he said to them, "You brood of vipers! Who warned you to flee from the wrath to come? Bear fruit worthy of repentance. Do not presume to say to yourselves, 'We have Abraham as our ancestor'; for I tell you, God is able from these stones to raise up children to Abraham. Even now the ax is lying at the root of the trees; every tree therefore that does not bear good fruit is cut down and thrown into the fire." (Matt 3:7–10)

One tribal narrative that has particular power today is the narrative of nationalism, particularly Christian, ethnic nationalism. This narrative ideology promotes the interests of a particular form of ethnic, religious, and/or cultural identity within our nation. Let's be clear, service to our nation can elicit wonderful feelings of patriotism and sacrifice. Being patriotic is a strong expression of group solidarity. But pride comes before the fall, especially when ethnonationalism goes beyond God's commandments and aims to divide rather than unite. Instead of God being above all things, the nation and its symbols emerge on top. The same can be applied to family, ethnic, or cultural groups who form bonds of solidarity in opposition to other groups in the neighborhood. Racism and white supremacy have their roots in this kind of narrow story of identity and triumphant tribalism.

Triumphant tribalism thrives around the world in many ways. When it emerges, it leads to destruction and violence. Since the brain and our biological makeup are hardwired to fear "strangers," tribal stories can easily lead to violence against and oppression of "the others." Triumphant tribalism becomes particularly toxic when mixed and identified with Christian faithfulness. True Christians must never be defined by their membership in or loyalty to a particular tribe. Many of our brothers and sisters in Germany fell to the temptation of Christian nationalism during the Second World War. This experience is a reminder of the dangers of triumphant tribalism and a call to all Christians, and perhaps Lutherans in particular, to wave the warning flag against this form of assault on the gospel.

I have seen the negative impact the four worldviews or counterstories described above continue to have on most Christian congregations today. These stories have become for many Christians their preferred "architecture"—that is, the spiritual homes in which they live and the foundations on which these homes are built. But following the parable's warning, building on these is like the "foolish man who built his house on sand" (Matt 7:26). Economic stories, religious stories, and tribal/cultural stories can quickly eclipse the Christian story when no other avenue is found to connect faith and economics. That's the bottom line: These alternative worldviews can colonize true discipleship and claim to be true Christian teaching. How do we defend ourselves from the idolatry that these counternarratives present to the Christian story? By learning to tell God's economic story well.

TELLING THE OLD, OLD STORY WELL

I propose that one way to counter these false narratives is through teaching Luther's *Small Catechism*, a dynamic summary of the Christian that emerged from Luther's visits among his people in 1528. Luther wrote the catechism to address the counternarratives in his day that had weakened the knowledge of the gospel among both laity and clergy. In this simple but profound resource, Luther provides the basics of God's story of redemption with all its implications for your faith, your vocational life, and your economic life.

As a Christian leader, I was allowing too much space for all four counternarratives among my people. By not connecting Sunday and Monday, I was letting certain economic stories infiltrate the lives of my people, from permitting the inner allure of the prosperity message to seep in, to allowing people to get stuck in MTD, to tolerating others hanging tribal flags higher in the sanctuaries of their daily lives than the cross of Christ. Even homo economicus roamed the pews without challenge. A lot is at stake in learning how to tell the gospel story so that our fellow Christians can hear and tell it for themselves in ways that bridge the gap between Sunday and Monday.

THE *SMALL CATECHISM*'S RESPONSE TO FALSE NARRATIVES

Telling the gospel story well always includes exposing counternarratives. Luther's evangelical catechism addresses those mentioned here and others, and it does so by unpacking an eight-sided message about how God functions in the world. The Triune God acts, for Luther, in the ways captured by the various parts of the *Small Catechism*:

- The Ten Commandments regulate all of life and lead us to recognize our need for God's presence in all aspects of our lives. They call out "idolatry" as a threat against those aspects of our lives that seek to fill that ultimate need, be they nation, culture, race, family, money, prosperity, or property. They call us to serve our neighbor and warn us about a life turned in on itself in self-interest rather than outward toward service.
- The Apostles' Creed reminds us of the triune nature of God, who creates, redeems, and sustains us and all things. We are reminded that God's work of creation calls us to work in and for creation. We are reminded of Jesus's work of forgiveness and redemption, of his triumph over the forces of sin, death, and the power of the devil. And we are reminded of how God's economy is powered by the Holy Spirit, guiding eighth-day disciples in the task of renewing this world.
- The Lord's Prayer teaches us how to live into this new life in Christ's kingdom, a kingdom that touches every aspect of our lives. It defines what the kingdom is and what it is not. The prayer teaches us to focus on the eighth day of creation, reflecting the core dimensions of the life of faith.

The movement from the Ten Commandments to the Apostles' Creed to the Lord's Prayer is Luther's way of defining the evangelical experience. Like a waltz, being evangelical involves learning and then dancing this spiritual three-step. Faith depends on this narrative flow to the story. Luther summarized the basic "evangelical" three-step movement of the catechism with an analogy from the medical field:

- The commandments show us the need for major surgery.
- The Apostles' Creed represents the major surgery that fixes our malady.
- The Lord's Prayer is the medicine we take daily after surgery to promote good health in the kingdom.[22]

Being grounded in the eight chapters of the catechism provides a counternarrative to the destructive stories that surround us and try to influence us every day. These eight tools can also lead to Christian spiritual practices that touch our work and our economic relationships.

CONCLUSION

My theological education assumed a divorce between Sunday and Monday, a chasm between worship and work, a rift between the sacred and the secular, and a gap as wide as the Grand Canyon between spirituality and economics. More problematic, I was comfortable with this divorce. Even though my Lutheran tradition had teachings that could have broadened my horizons, I overlooked them. I just didn't see the implications of Martin Luther's twin teachings on justification and vocation. I didn't seem to need these ideas for doing congregational ministry. The priesthood of all believers as a teaching of the Reformation was affirmed, of course. Who could be opposed to it as a Protestant? It was the churchly equivalent of American values like "Mom" and "apple pie." But concerning its importance for my ministry, however, I was clueless. The implications for economics were likewise lost on me. The Reformation had but one pillar: justification

alone! Economics as a theological focus was nonexistent. I was satis-
fied with the Sabbath-day ministries of rest. I didn't have a theology
of work.

Then came major disruptions for workers in my congregation.
Economic hardships grew. So many were riding the roller coaster of
the modern workplace. The coronavirus disrupted lives. The storms
were getting more frequent. I was realizing that Monday through
Saturday were the days when discipleship—and thus the mission of
God's people—had to be practiced. The architecture that defined discipleship for those days of the week needed to have an eight-sided
design, just like that ancient basilica in Philippi.

It's to Luther's insights in the *Small Catechism* that we will turn to
next to see how this five-hundred-year-old gem can help us live the
eighth-day story today in "the real world."

4

The Catechism and the Ten Commandments

Law as the First Key to an Evangelical Design

> Their de facto position is that Americans must die for the Dow.
> —Paul Krugman, "How Long Will It Take for the Economy to Recover?," *New York Times*, May 21, 2020

> "Of course, everybody wants to save every life they can, but the question is: Toward what end, ultimately?" . . . "The economic devastation is equally sad."
> —Chris Christie, interview with Dana Bash, CNN, May 5, 2020

The three previous chapters focused on eighth-day discipleship and the importance of telling the gospel story in ways that connect the Christian faith with work and economics. Why? Because without these connections, discipleship becomes irrelevant in God's economy. Spirituality remains abstract and lives in the clouds without integrating these central dimensions in our lives. Furthermore, without connecting faith, work, and economics, Christian formation will leave people vulnerable and susceptible to counternarratives. Damage will ensue. The confession that "Jesus is Lord" encompasses all of life. Work and economics must then find their place in relationship to faith. Jesus's Lordship invites us to embrace the all-encompassing, redemptive story of the eighth day of creation, which includes finding ourselves in God's home economics project. We turn now to the church's catechism to see what it can teach us about discipleship and the eighth day of creation while continuing to use the elements of faith, work, and economics as guides.

ENCOUNTERING THE CATECHISM FOR THE FIRST TIME

I started studying the catechism, as is typical for Lutherans, at the age of thirteen. To be clear, when I first opened the catechism, I had little interest in the twin topics of work and economics. My driving interests were girls and sports. Consequently, work and economics did not provide any meaningful context for my catechetical lessons. My only notion of a "call" came as a young boy when I visited Memorial Stadium in Baltimore to watch the Orioles play. Every time I laid my eyes on that field, I "knew" I had been called to be a professional baseball player. At that time, I couldn't imagine how the catechism could assist me in discerning a "call" in my life, whether to baseball or anything else.

My father, now in his second parish, taught my confirmation class at Trinity Lutheran Church in Norfolk, Virginia. Confirmation was a two-year program and taught on Saturday mornings. The catechetical instruction was serious and thorough. In other words, German. Like Elijah challenging the prophets of Baal on Mount Carmel, these Saturday classes were meant to force students to choose between church and school activities (read: sports). I was athletic, so the choice represented an existential crisis. Sensing my wavering spiritual commitment, my father informed me of the "right" choice. Saturday mornings now were reserved for confirmation class.

The Saturday sessions revolved around the eight parts of the catechism. Like the catechism itself, the sessions mostly involved questions and answers related to the given topic of the day. Ultimately, this instruction was intended to prepare the class for a final oral exam where we would be marched before the elders of the church and grilled about our faith. This meant being "capable of confirming your faith with adequate substance and conviction." There were 258 questions on the oral exam and ten kids in my class. We had done the math. Each confirmation student would have to answer 25.8 questions. I still sweat a little whenever I remember standing before those church elders.

Reflecting on the whole confirmation experience, I must admit, it was a positive one. The process was extremely formative to my personal and spiritual development. But it also left a false impression that after the final oral exam, I would "graduate." I assumed that passing that exam was a rite of passage in becoming an adult, and after, I could finally put away the catechism safely in a drawer until I had children of my own. My children could then be sent to confirmation classes with my old catechism in tow. Nostalgic!

Naturally, the reason we memorized the eight parts of the catechism was so that we would "own" its content. I get that now. When I was thirteen, though, memorization was a subtle form of spiritual torture. Now I know that memorization means ownership. Memorized content stands always ready and available. Was this general conviction embraced more broadly within the congregation? I ask this question because I never heard adults at church quote from the catechism. Could the majority even recite all Ten Commandments by heart? The result of these unspoken attitudes was clear: the catechism's content was for the formation of children, not adults.

I have since learned that the older we get, the more we need the catechism. This little book summarizes Scripture. Its pages encourage discipleship, especially for adults. This insight about "the catechism for adults" has only come recently. Just a few years ago when I needed to find connections between faith, work, and economics for my own life, I didn't immediately turn to the catechism. Luther's *Small Catechism* was primarily for children and newer Christians, I thought. As a result, I simply overlooked a fundamental resource for making essential connections between faith and daily life.

In 2012, the topics of "work" and "economics" as they related to the gospel story had begun to capture my imagination. Questions about economics and work started to grow in importance as I posed the following questions:

- Are faith, work, and economics modern topics, or did Reformers already address them back in the sixteenth century?
- Was my Reformation tradition in this regard a source of treasure to be mined, or must I go to other traditions to strike gold?
- Can the catechism deal with adult issues in forming eighth-day disciples?

To address these questions, I decided to read the Lutheran church's discipleship manual to discover what it might say on these topics, if anything. If Martin Luther addressed them at all, he would have included them in his discipleship handbook from 1529, the *Small Catechism*. That was my logic.

LUTHER'S *SMALL CATECHISM*—SOME HISTORY

Within the Lutheran tradition, Luther's *Small Catechism* has been used to disciple Christians for five hundred years. Many Lutherans across the world have memorized the *Small Catechism* word for word and studied it in detail. The catechism's contents have remained essentially the same since 1529, after Luther conducted a broad visitation of evangelical parishes under his supervision. What he discovered shocked him. He referred to the state of people's lives as "wretched deprivation." Luther's language was always colorful. As Professor Jon Pahl points out, "By this phrase 'wretched deprivation' Luther does not mean only that congregants lacked theological sophistication. . . . Some of the first examples of what Luther intended were economic."[1] Economic?!

Luther recommended that parents and leaders in the church teach the catechism and "put the greatest stress on that commandment or part where your people experience the greatest need. For example, you must strongly emphasize the Seventh Commandment, dealing with stealing, to artisans and shopkeepers and even to farmers and household workers, because rampant among such people are all kinds of dishonesty and thievery (BC 349)."[2] The *Small Catechism* was Luther's attempt to disciple his people after discovering their struggles in daily life.

Luther's response to the spiritual crisis was both substantive and strategic. He decided to create discipleship centers, the most primary of which was the home. Parents were called to lead their families and workers (because the home is a place of business too) by discipling them. The *Small Catechism* was written and designed to be the tool placed into their hands. Pastors and teachers would undergird, support, and encourage this catechetical training. The church actually "called" parents to this home ministry. This call for parents to raise their families in faith began with their public promise at the baptismal font. Their responsibilities were laid out there in detail. Discipleship training was a high call for any parent.

Luther's *Small Catechism* contains eight essential parts: the Ten Commandments, the Apostles' Creed, the Lord's Prayer, baptism, communion, confession (the Office of the Keys), blessings, and the Table of Duties. In many ways, Luther's *Small Catechism* reflected the standard structure and practice of catechetical writings from the earliest times until the sixteenth century. The question-and-answer format was common. This small book defined how discipleship was taught among the newly formed evangelicals, but it did so by using an old format.

The reasons for Christians of all persuasions to explore this particular catechism as a discipleship tool, even if they are not Lutheran, are simple:

1. Luther's *Small Catechism* is one of the oldest discipleship manuals for Protestants.
2. Its structure and theology are together one of the best examples of Luther's evangelical theology.
3. The booklet has been essentially unchanged for five hundred years.
4. It teaches the faith using work (i.e., vocation) and economic terms.

5.   The catechism tells a story and invites you to enter that story
by faith.

The point about work and economics was for me the biggest surprise. This Reformation text is packed with vocational and economic
terms.[3] Theologians today affirm that work and economics are referred
to explicitly throughout Luther's catechisms.[4] For example, Luther's
favorite term for salvation—*redemption*—is an economic one. Furthermore, as we will see, his catechism is dominated by vocational
language, starting with the commandments. For Luther, the catechism loses much of its context and power as a discipleship manual
without this understanding of vocation. This may be one reason children in their early teens today have a hard time grasping the depth of
the catechism and why adults get it immediately.

What had Luther observed that I had missed? That's what I hoped
to discover in his *Small Catechism*. What happened over those five
hundred years to change evangelical approaches to discipleship? The
questions again started to pile up.

The three classic pillars of all catechisms—the Ten Commandments, the Apostles' Creed, and the Lord's Prayer—are the basic
elements of the evangelical story. In this chapter, we focus on the Ten
Commandments.

THE TEN COMMANDMENTS AS THE FIRST TOOL
FOR SPIRITUAL FORMATION

Luther's catechism, like most catechisms before it, was built on three
fundamental pillars of the faith. The order of presentation was always
the same before the Reformation: creed, commandments, and the
Lord's Prayer. Such an order remains the same even today, for example, for Roman Catholics, Anglicans, Presbyterians, and some evangelical congregations. To make this point more concrete, ask yourself,
In learning the faith, what came first in your instruction?

Telling the gospel story "evangelically," for Luther, meant changing
this order. A small change but a big result. Luther wanted to preserve

the grace-based character of the gospel of Jesus Christ. So Luther rearranged the classic three pillars by starting with the Ten Commandments instead of the Apostles' Creed. God's law came first, for Luther, and then the good news about the Triune God (creed). Law before gospel. More about the importance of this shift later, because it has major implications for how we approach work and economics within the framework of eighth-day discipleship. For the present, however, Luther's answer about which pillar of the faith to address first was clear: we start with the Ten Commandments. Let's look then at the commandments to explore what they can teach us, and then how they help us tell the gospel story about the eighth day of creation.

GOD'S LAW AND THE EIGHTH DAY OF CREATION

Luther's catechism begins with the list of commandments used by Saint Augustine in the fourth and fifth centuries (353 to 430 CE). Luther had options. The Bible lists the "Ten Commandments" three times in its first five books: in Exodus 20, Deuteronomy 5, and Leviticus 19. These biblical lists differ slightly. Consequently, churches have had choices in how they edit and number the Ten Commandments. Every church tradition edits the biblical lists to get to ten. But the way they edit these lists speaks volumes about how they understand the role the commandments play within the big story of the eighth day of creation.

Almost all churches teach the importance of the commandments, but these teachings differ. Speaking in broad terms, five Christian traditions dominate how people have been taught to use the Ten Commandments. Before reading Luther's approach (the fifth), try to identify how you have been taught to use the commandments in your daily life, at work, home, and school.

Fundamentalists/Literalists

Fundamentalists believe in a literal reading of the commandments. All commandments in the Bible are God's word, have equal importance, and should be obeyed (including all 613 laws of the Torah). A Christian must obey all biblical laws because the Bible is the inerrant word of God. Some fundamentalists make distinctions between the Old and the New Testaments or ritual and moral laws. In general, however, God's law never changes, and it must be obeyed as written.

Natural Law / Virtues

Roman Catholics read the commandments in the Bible and recognize that a literal reading isn't plausible. The commandments are complicated. Roman Catholics respect the tradition of natural law, which sees moral order as corresponding to God's created order (see Rom 1). Conforming to God's moral order in the world represents the virtuous life. Thus, Roman Catholics interpret the commandments through the authority of the church, in response to various contexts and in light of the created order, with emphasis placed on striving to live virtuously in response to God's word. Grace and love empower Christians to obey the commandments.

God-Given Instinct for Moral Justice

These Protestants, often found in mainline churches, also respond negatively to a literal reading of the commandments. They do so, however, by using God-given instincts for justice. These Christians find many of the biblical laws and commandments antiquated or just wrong (because of, for example, slavery and gender issues). They use the commandments to highlight their God-given sense of justice in today's world. They too refer to Paul's "law in the heart" in Romans 1. A holy sense of justice and mercy is therefore paramount and drives their moral and ethical practice. God's moral law for today is evolving as the Holy Spirit draws us more deeply into the divine call for love, justice, and mercy in our personal lives and structurally in society.

Moral and Biblical Principles / Reflecting God's Character

Evangelicals use their moral instincts as well to interpret the command-ments. These instincts are tied closely to the biblical text. Evangelicals speak of the commandments in the human heart following Paul in Romans 1. They also speak of character formation—that is, Christians striving for a Christlike character. "Biblical principles" are taken from God's laws. Sometimes distinctions are made between ritual and moral laws, Old and New Testament laws, and between biblical texts to be highlighted and those that should be simply overlooked. God's laws train us to reflect a godlike character through the work of the Holy Spirit. Salvation in Christ makes following the moral and ethical laws possible.

Law as Formation and a Prelude to Faith

Lutherans teach that God's law ultimately leads us to the knowl-edge of sin and the need for Christ. That's its chief purpose. The law forms us like a disciplinarian or a schoolteacher. But fulfilling the law isn't the goal of faith formation. Faith in Christ is the goal. Ultimately, faith means freedom from the law. Lutherans take the Ten Commandments seriously as a summary of natural law. But biblical commandments, mandates, principles, and virtues are merely tools that reflect God's law as it is built into the natural order. They are secondary, not primary, for discipleship. Yes, the law does serve a positive purpose in society by setting up rules that create conditions of trust among people. The Ten Commandments, however, ultimately condemn us. Laws dis-cipline, they contain a curse, and they kill (Gal 3 and Rom 7). The gos-pel frees. Only the life of faith pleases God and enables the Christian to live life with freedom and responsibility.

To summarize, different traditions use the commandments differently. This should not be a surprise. Law regulates life. There are more ref-erences in the Bible to laws concerning economic issues than prayer. How should a Christian read the biblical commandments and God's law vis-à-vis their work or economic life? These questions will shape a Christian's worldview. They will determine how to bridge the gap between Sunday and Monday. Eighth-day discipleship begins with the commandments as God's law.

A LUTHERAN APPROACH TO THE LAW

Luther presents the Ten Commandments within his *Small Catechism* as the first place to bridge the gap between Sunday and Monday. He does so with a few theological assumptions about how God's law functions and how it leads to faith, freedom, and responsibility. Here is a list of some of these key assumptions, presented within my own categorical frameworks:

- *God's word comes as two words, not one.* The word of God comes to people as two words—God's law to obey and God's promise to believe. Discipleship therefore begins with grasping the law of God. The gospel, as the second word, can only be good news for a person once one is grasping and being grasped by God's law.[5]
- *The Ten Commandments reflect God's orderly creation.* For Luther, the Ten Commandments were a summary of natural law. The universe has a moral and ethical order at its core. Because they are part of the created order, the commandments have their original home not on slabs of stone (i.e., Moses's) but in the human heart (Jer 31 and Rom 1), in humanity as a whole, and in the world. Luther makes a sharp distinction between the commandments as a summary of the natural law versus the specific commands given to Moses and the Hebrew people at Sinai.[6] We aren't to obey the laws given to Moses. They were for Moses. We are to obey the natural law built into the created order.
- *The law is a gift and a burden.* The knowledge of good and evil, which resides in our conscience, was not originally a gift to humans from God. This knowledge, which we also can call

"moral knowledge," comes on account of human rebellion against God. In one sense, it helps us recognize evil, which protects us from its effects. But the law is also a burden we must now bear. The law reminds us that our moral knowledge is partial, fuzzy, and corrupt. Our relationship with God is clouded. Consequently, we have the "knowledge of good and evil" (Gen 3), but our understanding is incomplete. The law therefore is a gift and burden. Laws help us. But they can't solve the "sin problem." Laws can never fulfill God's demand to love.

- *Laws are leaves and leather.* The story of the fall within the garden of Eden is instructive in describing how the law functions. Laws don't solve problems; they cover them up. After the fall, Adam and Eve experienced sin and shame, which disturbed their work and economic life. They decided to address their vulnerability by covering their nakedness. Their "cover-up" started with leaves. Obviously, this first attempt at a fashion statement was only partially successful. The clothes shriveled. Shame grew. So God mercifully showed them how to make better clothes, using the newest technology found in the garden, leather (Gen 3). Clothes didn't solve Adam and Eve's problem, but clothes did help make work and economic activity possible outside the garden.

- *Moral law acts as a curb, rule, mirror, and X-ray machine.* Luther spoke of two uses of the law: the civil (or first) use of the law and the spiritual (or second) use of the law. Civil use is the curb and rule. The Ten Commandments teach us how to construct a trustworthy world in which people can play and work together safely, without outbreaks of sin, chaos, and disorder. Laws teach us how to work and construct a relatively just economic order that serves the neighbor. Moral law isn't perfect, but it defines what it's like to do two things—don't break stuff and promote the common good. This is the law's civic role. In doing this, however, the law also plays a spiritual role as both a mirror and an X-ray machine. Law reflects the

truth that we're naked before God and other people. Law
exposes injustice. Law reveals sin. Finally, the law condemns
and "kills" us.

- *Laws are communal.* Laws are discovered within communities. This is particularly true when we discuss communities
  through the lens of economic relationships—that is, the
  system of exchange-creating relationships between people.
  Luther was clear that the law calls us to responsible action in
  the world through at least four communities: family, work,
  civil, and religious.[7] All the dos and don'ts of the Ten Commandments, and all the rights and responsibilities that come
  with these laws, are discovered, experienced, and lived out
  in the various communities, contexts, and cultures in which
  we live.

THE TEN COMMANDMENTS

Now that we have reviewed some of Luther's teachings concerning
the law, we turn to the Ten Commandments as Luther laid them out
in the *Small Catechism*. In doing so, we want to highlight references
to "work" and "economics." The *Small Catechism* is telling a story. So
we must constantly explore what role the commandments play within
this evangelical story of the eighth day of creation.

The summary of the Ten Commandments is quite simple—love
God and neighbor. These two love mandates summarize the two
tablets or tables of the law. The cliff-notes version of Moses's law is
summarized when a lawyer in Luke's Gospel confronts Jesus with
this question: "'Teacher,' he said, 'what must I do to inherit eternal
life?' He said to him, 'What is written in the law? What do you read
there?' He answered, 'You shall love the Lord your God with all your
heart, and with all your soul, and with all your strength, and with
all your mind; and your neighbor as yourself.' And he said to him,
'You have given the right answer; do this, and you will live'" (Luke
10:25–28).

The First Table of the Law: Love God

We begin, therefore, with the first table of the law, which focuses on loving God. We will list these laws, making references to how Luther understands them vis-à-vis vocational and economic issues. Luther lays out each command and then follows it up with a question. It's like he is instructing a three-year-old child who answers every question with another question: What is *that*?! (or, What does this mean?).[8]

In short, I will organize each section in the same way that Luther organized the catechism. First comes the commandment itself. After the commandment comes Luther's explanation of its meaning in response to the question "*What is this?* or *What does this mean?*"[9] Finally, I will add a brief commentary, lifting up key dimensions of the commandment that touch on the topics of faith, work, and economics (FWE). Our goal in outlining the catechism in this way is to see how Luther's approach to discipleship reflects on the eighth day of creation story as he makes explicit connections among faith, work, and economics.

The First Commandment
You shall have no other gods.

What is this? or *What does this mean?*
We are to fear, love, and trust God above all things.

FWE Commentary
God is above all things; this includes our family, work, civic life, the environment, and all our "garden economies." There is no secular or sacred divide here, no division between personal and public, Sunday and Monday activities. "Work" must not run our lives, and neither should "rest," money, the economy, or anything else. Being a "workaholic" is exposed as making work into an idol. Work can dominate to the detriment of all the other dimensions of our lives. The biggest temptation in a free market is to place the economy on the pedestal

as the ultimate god. Idolatry is placing our ultimate trust in something aside from God. Economic gods may include profit, retirement accounts, the stock market, the accumulation of property, employment, a paycheck, tax revenue, or market growth. These are all good things. But they are forbidden from being forces that run our lives. We are commanded to fear, love, and trust in God above all things.

One of the biggest temptations in our economy is to serve the god of prosperity, economic growth, and global economic progress. These forces quickly become golden calves, like those of the children of Israel in the wilderness. "Many economists believe in progress in a religious way, as something that is significantly improving the basic human condition for the better,"[10] or, represented another way, "Every age has its illusions. Ours has been this fervent belief in the power of prosperity."[11] By not trusting in God above all things, we either fear scarcity in our lives or seek ultimate security in prosperity's fruits.

The ultimate spiritual enemy is economic idolatry, which reduces life to power or a bottom line of profits and losses. By placing our trust in an economic god, we can quickly lose our humanity. The parable of the rich fool in Luke looms large over our lives (Luke 12:13–21). "That this economic reading of the first commandment is consistent with Luther's intent becomes clear in the Large Catechism"; in short, in Luther's catechism, critique of economic idolatry is the first and most crucial point.[12]

Luther writes,

> So that it may be understood and remembered, I must explain this a little more plainly by citing some everyday examples of the opposite [of fearing and loving, and trusting God above all things]. There are some who think that they have God and everything they need when they have money and property; they trust in them and boast in them so stubbornly and securely that they care for no one else. They, too, have a god—mammon by name, that is, money and property—on which they set their whole heart. This is the most common idol on earth.[13]

Work can become a god. It happens quickly. This idol will often tempt us to give up everything else in our lives except the office. The same is true for work's twin, economics. It's not hard to see when economic forces become idols in other people's lives. We observe this idolatry daily in the marketplace. It angers us. We are confronted with it everywhere, and the "love of money is a root of all kinds of evil" (1 Tim 6:10). The challenge is to avoid these forms of idolatry ourselves.

The Second Commandment
You shall not make wrongful use of the name of the Lord your God.

What is this? or *What does this mean?*
We are to fear and love God, so that we do not curse, swear, practice magic, lie, or deceive using God's name, but instead use that very name in every time of need to call on, pray, praise, and give thanks to God.

FWE Commentary
God's name is to be kept holy, not to be exploited or misused for familial, work, political, national, or economic gain. This commandment has often been applied within the context of legal courts. Today, its application to business and to the church itself is even more relevant. Again, Luther makes this economic reading clearer in the *Large Catechism*, where he writes, "Misuse of the divine name occurs first of all in business affairs and in matters involving money and property."[14] As Jon Pahl adds, "After all, gratitude and trust is the foundation of every contract, cooperative effort, and policy; unless language is secure, nothing truly human happens."[15]

When it comes to your work and your economic concerns, let your "yes" be yes, and your "no" be no, says Jesus in the Sermon on the Mount (Matt 5:37). Christians should not leverage God's name for business advantage. Using heavenly endorsements to promote earthly business is crossing a dangerous line. The same is true, for national affairs, with claims that "God is on our side." This danger of claiming God's allegiance for "our side" looms large in business, economics, work, sports, politics, and religion, but this commandment's prohibition rings clear: "Don't do it!"

We preach and teach a gospel that offers God's promise of grace to the world in Christ without cost or price. God's favor in Christ is received by faith—that is, without indulgences paid to the church, financial contributions as down payments for blessings, demands for generosity as a necessary proof of one's faith, or the planting of "seed faith" in ministry coffers to gain God's financial or spiritual favor at a later date. We don't drop the divine name to leverage economic or political advantage. God's name is not to be used for personal or collective gain. God's name is to be used for prayer, praise, thanksgiving, and blessing the world that God so loves.

The Third Commandment
Remember the sabbath day, and keep it holy.

What is this? or *What does this mean?*
We are to fear and love God, so that we do not despise preaching or God's word, but instead keep that word holy and gladly hear and learn it.

FWE Commentary
In Luther's era, as in our own, people worked on Friday and Saturday, literally on the Sabbath day. Just transferring the Sabbath to another day of the week, Sunday, is not really respecting the commandment in a literal sense. The important thing for Luther was that this law did not apply to Christians at all, since, for Christians, God's word sanctifies every day of the week. So what is all the anxiety around choosing between Saturday or Sunday as the true Sabbath? For that matter, why not choose Wednesday?

Luther takes the word of God seriously. He focuses on a double sense of "rest" in this Sabbath commandment. That includes rest for workers from their labors and spiritual "rest," which Luther says comes from hearing the word of God, especially in community. The rhythm of work and rest should reflect our participation in God's life of creation—that is, God worked and rested. We work and rest. How God rests and works defines God's stewardship of all creation. No day better models this relation between rest and work than Sunday. Sunday will then be a model for Monday.

One of the greatest differences between ancient Roman law and Jewish law was that for Romans, the land and all its wealth belonged to its citizens. People owned land, wealth, and slaves, and they could do with them as they pleased. It was their right. In Jewish law, in contrast, God owns the land and wealth. God calls God's people to steward what is ultimately God's. This stewardship involves "rest" and "work." Within God's ownership, God designates "rights" to the land, to the slave, to the dispossessed, to the poor, and to the land itself. These rights often center on the teaching of Sabbath rest and Sabbath work.[16] Our hearing of God's word is what keeps us therefore participating in God's very life as stewards of what belongs to God. Even our rest glorifies God and celebrates God's six-day work of creation. This rest also recognizes our own work and rest as direct participation in the life of God. Sabbath rest prepares us for the work of the eighth day of creation (the discussion of eighth-day work comes in the next sections on the Apostles' Creed and the Lord's Prayer).

The Second Table of the Law: Love the Neighbor

Whereas the first table of the law above—the first three commandments—focused our attention on love of God, the second table of the law focuses on how to love and serve the neighbor. Whereas the first table of the law emerged from the power of the First Commandment, commandants four to ten flow from the power of the Fourth Commandment. Interestingly, Luther interprets the Fourth Commandment as the "vocation commandment." All other commandments flow through and are framed by our various calls and responsibilities for serving the neighbor.

The Fourth Commandment
Honor your father and your mother.

What is this? or *What does this mean?*
We are to fear and love God, so that we neither despise nor anger our parents and others in authority, but instead honor, serve, obey, love, and respect them.

FWE Commentary
The Fourth Commandment for Luther is the "vocation command-ment." It includes behavioral and attitudinal service to all neighbors, not just our parents. For Luther, the meaning of the commandment is extended to honoring all those in authority over us, including parents; bosses; service professionals; civic, political, and religious leaders; and more. On the flip side, this commandment affirms the vocations of parents, workers, citizens, and members of the body of Christ as you serve and love your neighbor: "Vocation clarifies moral issues. . . . Vocations come with their respective responsi-bilities, and they also come with authority, to the point that some actions are sinful when done outside of a particular vocation but good when done within that vocation." Obvious examples are sol-diers and judges.[17]

Roles tied to our vocations are critical for Luther because he sees the world sacramentally. This means that God is loving the world through you and through your work. More specifically, God is lov-ing the world through the "offices" or positions you've been given to serve the neighbor. Luther calls these "the masks of God." The lan-guage here is from the theater. An actor wears a mask on stage. When you look behind any work or vocational activity that we carry out in the world, when you take away the mask, you see God at work. Concerning the notion of God's masks, Gene Veith writes, "Accord-ing to Luther, vocation is a 'mask of God' (Commentary on Psalm 147, LW 14:114). God is milking the cows through the vocation of the milkmaid, said Luther. He is hidden in vocation. We see the milkmaid or the farmer or the doctor of the pastor or the artist. But, looming behind this human mask, God is genuinely present and active in what they do for us."[18]

Since Christ has given you God's favor without any work or merit on your part, your life is now dedicated to serving the neighbor. This commandment affirms your various vocations in life, the ways God calls you to serve the neighbor, as well as affirming the neighbor's vocations for serving you. Whether Christian or not, these "calls" or offices of service are built into the fabric of creation. God designed the world to work this way. The notion of "vocation" points to the architecture of creation, God's economy. Teaching about our work and our economic lives should first flow from this commandment on vocation. This commandment orders and regulates all of life around service and sacrifice by establishing vocational lines of authority.

Finally, let's not forget parents in this larger vocational picture. For many of us, our parents are our closest and dearest "neighbors." Honoring them acknowledges their special "call" in our lives.

The Fifth Commandment
You shall not murder.

What is this? or *What does this mean?*
We are to fear and love God, so that we neither endanger nor harm the lives of our neighbors, but instead help and support them in all of life's needs.

FWE Commentary
The Fifth Commandment involves behavior or service aimed at protecting and defending your neighbor's basic bodily needs. So the commandment to honor all vocations is followed by the commandment to protect your neighbor's physical well-being. Luther's interpretation of this commandment has strong economic implications. It's like Luther knows Maslow's hierarchy of needs. Your neighbor's physical needs come first. The reference to "all life's needs" refers to our basic physical needs in life. These bodily needs include food, shelter,

adequate clothing, health care, and protection from physical abuse. Luther sums it up this way: "God wants to have everyone defended, delivered, and protected from the wickedness and violence of others, and he has placed this commandment as a wall, fortress, and refuge around our neighbors, so that no one may do them bodily harm or injury."[19]

Luther's examples are usually economic in nature and include acts of both commission and omission: "If you send a naked person away when you could clothe him, you have let him freeze to death. If you see anyone who is suffering from hunger and do not feed her, you have let her starve."[20]

Within a traditional agricultural context, this commandment also refers to livestock. Don't let this rural reference fool you. Livestock represents your capital, your family's property and savings, your investments, and your 401K. Old Testament law is clear that if your bull (i.e., your asset) hurts your neighbor, you are responsible.[21] That kind of violence is a "capital" offense, at least if you were warned first of the danger. The lesson is that your capital, assets, and property need to be dealt with if they are hurting your neighbor and causing physical harm. Analogously, this same principle applies to one's investment portfolio in a free market economy. Your investments and holdings must also be serving the neighbor, not causing physical harm.

The Sixth Commandment
You shall not commit adultery.

What is this? or *What does this mean?*
We are to fear and love God, so that we lead pure and decent lives in word and deed, and each of us loves and honors his or her spouse.

FWE Commentary
The Sixth Commandment involves behavior and service focused on leading a sexually pure life with all neighbors and especially with one's

spouse or partner. Within a marriage, your closest neighbor to love and serve is your partner. The family is the basis of our economic system as a nation. The family's economic health is the bedrock of both the community at large and the nurturing and procreation of children. There's a lot at stake for the health of a society in having healthy, thriving families. Sexual purity and fidelity are the best ways to guard and promote marriage and family life. By serving and honoring our partners and families, we better the wider community. A trustworthy family life creates an environment of trust within the wider community and promotes a solid basis for all other economic activities outside the home. Furthermore, because our identities are so wrapped up with our sexuality, violating sexual barriers creates mistrust, hurt, pain, and damage among friends and neighbors, especially work colleagues. Building trust in family, work, and community without respecting sexual boundaries is impossible.

The Seventh Commandment
You shall not steal.

What is this? or *What does this mean?*
We are to fear and love God, so that we neither take our neighbors' money or property nor acquire them by using shoddy merchandise or crooked deals, but instead help them to improve their property and income.

FWE Commentary
The Seventh Commandment focuses on service to the neighbor by respecting the neighbor's possessions and property. The economic implications of this commandment are straightforward: don't take or defraud, but help, guard, and protect your neighbor's stuff and livelihood. Economic competition is not forbidden in this commandment, especially if one "competes" to serve and love the neighbor in a more efficient and faithful manner, modeling sacrifice. But greed and theft are forbidden.

Greed is idolatry. It is failing to believe in God. A distinction is often made in the medieval church between theft and greed. Theft in canon law recognized the person who stole to keep food on the table. This was wrong, but greed was worse. Greed represents an insatiable appetite. It is addictive in character, always grabbing for more. Luther had little difficulty speaking truth to power when it came to greed in politics or business: "These [thieves] sit in their chairs and are known as great lords and honorable, upstanding citizens while they rob and steal under the cloak of legality." Or when it came to politicians: "We might well keep quiet here about individual petty thieves since we ought to be attacking the great powerful arch thieves with whom lords and princes consort and who daily plunder not just a city or two, but all of Germany."[22] Naturally, political leaders were called to protect their people from "every evil." And yet, Luther argues, "I hear that [the princes] have a finger in [collusion with monopolies], and thus the saying of Isaiah [1:23] is fulfilled, 'Your princes have become companions of thieves.'"[23]

As numerous commentators have pointed out, Luther did not consider any social or professional class greedier than the others. He intended, instead, to identify and condemn greed by all members of all classes. It comes as no surprise, then, that in his commentaries on the Seventh Commandment, Luther speaks of the many who are plagued by greed: day laborers, workers, servants, artisans, burghers, butchers, shoemakers, farmers, tailors, beer makers, owners of trading monopolies, church leaders, magistrates, and princes. All persons face the challenge of this commandment. Regarding stealing, he says, "It should not be narrowly restricted, but it should pertain to anything that has to do with our neighbor."[24] Luther writes about this commandment to address both individual inclinations to steal as well as larger systemic theft within the economy: "Thievery is the most common craft and the largest guild on earth."[25]

Our call then is to reverse this self-serving trend by protecting our neighbor's property and business. This can be achieved even in a competitive economic environment. Competition-as-service doesn't have to give in to theft and greed to succeed and thrive. Service to neighbor must always be built on the freedom and dignity of the neighbor in all dealings.

The Eighth Commandment
You shall not bear false witness against your neighbor.

What is this? or *What does this mean?*
We are to fear and love God, so that we do not tell lies about our neighbors, betray or slander them, or destroy their reputations. Instead, we are to come to their defense, speak well of them, and interpret everything they do in the best possible light.

FWE Commentary
The Eighth Commandment focuses on service to neighbor through telling the truth and protecting their reputations. This commandment has become a real martyr in our present political and cultural environment. Our present practice is "cast aspersions first, apologize later (if at all)." Or "throw lies onto the wall, and see which ones stick." Innuendo and gossip reign as competitive techniques and tools of the trade in many fields. Fake news is employed for one simple reason: it works! Social media is a powerful tool that both builds and destroys reputations within a short amount of time. This commandment recognizes the treasure of a person's reputation and how it can affect their livelihood. If a person loses their reputation, they can lose their primary means for supporting their life. They may also lose their community. A reputation in business or within a family is a chief asset. This commandment prohibits hurting your neighbor's name or reputation, or their business's brand. Competition within the marketplace has its place in service to the neighbor, but bearing false witness to win a market share doesn't please God.

Instead, we are called to stay positive and put the best construction or spin on describing the neighbor and their business. Abuse of this commandment negatively impacts families, communities, or markets, sometimes affecting their very survival. No neighborhood or circle of friends can withstand the cancer of gossip. A workplace or school will be emotionally ruinous if it does not obey this commandment. And social media will ultimately collapse under its own oppressive weight if it ignores the Eighth Commandment.

The Ninth Commandment
You shall not covet your neighbor's house.

What is this? or *What does this mean?*
We are to fear and love God, so that we do not try to trick our neighbors out of their inheritance or property or try to get it for ourselves by claiming to have a legal right to it and the like, but instead be of help and service to them in keeping what is theirs.

FWE Commentary
The Ninth Commandment is a call for avoiding covetous thoughts regarding our neighbor's house and property, since thoughts can lead to action. It is fascinating to note that Luther listed the first "covet" commandment as the one that protects house and property. Since the children of Israel received land as their inheritance within the promised land, this commandment protected the inheritance and ownership of land, house, and property and prohibited schemes to undermine the neighbor's property and livelihood. Luther encourages us to protect the neighbor's house and property and avoid even entertaining legal schemes to take them. This commandment is one of the pillars of any free market economic system that works. Protecting private property promotes freedom and economic prosperity within a society. A family or business can only build equity and worth if homes and property are protected by laws. Schemes that trample on those rights are prohibited in this commandment. The same holds true for business competitors. The basis for any free market where families and businesses thrive is the respect for and execution of this commandment.

The Tenth Commandment

You shall not covet your neighbor's wife, or male or female slave, or
ox, or donkey, or anything that belongs to your neighbor.

What is this? or *What does this mean?*
We are to fear and love God, so that we do not entice, force, or steal
away from our neighbors their spouses, household workers, or livestock but instead urge them to stay and fulfill their responsibilities to
our neighbors.

FWE Commentary
The Tenth Commandment addresses attitudes toward the neighbor's
economic infrastructure, including spouse, workers, and assets. The
message is clear: don't desire anything that belongs to the neighbor. The language of this commandment is dated, coming out of a
male-oriented context. Its patriarchal framing may even be offensive,
but its intent is crystal clear. And its economic import is as relevant
today as it was in Moses's or Luther's day: Leave your neighbor's
things alone. Don't even entertain the notion of acquiring them in
an untoward manner. This commandment again recognizes the slip-
pery slope between attitudes and behaviors. Once we begin to covet
our neighbor's infrastructure (personal and financial) and their other
assets, behaviors will quickly follow suit. God demands in this commandment that we protect, support, and promote our neighbor's possessions, assets, and livelihood by restricting our desires so that our
neighbors can thrive and prosper without fear and anxiety.

This commandment also recognizes that our partners and family
relationships are some of our strongest economic assets. Don't covet,
therefore, any part of another person's family or relationships.

Conclusion to the Commandments

What then does God say about all these commandments?
God says the following: "I, the Lord your God, am a jealous God, punish-
ing children for the iniquity of parents, to the third and fourth generation

of those who reject me, but showing steadfast love to the thousandth generation of those who love me and keep my commandments."

What is this? or *What does this mean?*
God threatens to punish all who break these commandments. Therefore, we are to fear his wrath and not disobey these commandments. However, God promises grace and every good thing to all those who keep these commandments. Therefore, we also are to love and trust him and gladly act according to his commands.

FWE Commentary
How do we fulfill God's law? By loving God and serving the neighbor as worker-priests. We serve our neighbor by guarding and supporting their most basic needs, which include family relationships, economic needs, physical needs, and reputation. In so doing we extend the grace that we have received from God's generous hand.

Luther interprets the commandments with a strong vocational and economic focus. What the commandments teach us about work and economics, therefore, includes four basic lessons:

- God demands to be God. No idolatry will be tolerated. This includes the idolatry associated with our family, work, and economies.
- God wants our neighbors to thrive. To this end, God wants us to focus on serving our neighbor through our vocations or "callings to serve." These vocations are built into the fabric of creation. Our work matters.
- God commands us to serve our neighbor, especially regarding their economic well-being. Stealing, causing harm, committing adultery, gossiping, bearing false witness, and coveting or scheming to obtain the neighbor's house and property break down our relationship with our neighbor and society in general.
- God is loving the neighbor through our work. Life is not about self-interest. We are called as worker-priests. Life is sacramental in nature.

It is immediately evident that Martin Luther did not suffer from a divorce between Sunday and Monday. His *Small Catechism* was designed to teach discipleship in all of life, not just on Sunday. Daily work takes on dignity and even a sacramental quality through the practice of our "callings." We are called to be a nation of worker-priests from Monday through Saturday. Economic issues are also paramount in the commandments because without economics in the forefront, how would one possibly serve the neighbor in a meaningful and sustainable way? The commandments as God's law do set the tone for our work and economic relationships in the *Small Catechism*. Furthermore, as an overview of natural law, they are still in force.

In summary, the catechism suggests that any discussion of work and economics within the framework of eighth-day discipleship must start with God's commandments—God's concrete demands on our lives. These demands reflect God's natural moral order, no matter how fuzzy that order sometimes appears to us. God's order ultimately tells us the truth about ourselves: namely, that we can't keep to it. We miss the mark every time. Therefore, the first bridge between Sunday and Monday is the Ten Commandments.

It is important to note at this juncture the topics Luther hasn't yet addressed in the catechism: namely, redemption and the new creation in Christ. The eighth day of creation and resurrection life are not yet topics for discussion. Eighth-day issues come only after the commandments have done their dirty work of disclosure. Eighth-day realities come in the next two pillars of the catechism, and they will transform everything, even our grasp of the commandments.

However, the commandments set a framework for a trustworthy world. They are helpful and critical to our well-being, but they are no solution for our core problems of sin, shame, and nakedness. Law makes for an inadequate set of clothes to cover our nakedness. Leather and leaves, ultimately, are lousy solutions to our deeper problem. Redemption, summarized in the Apostles' Creed, will offer God's ultimate solution to sin.

5

The Catechism and Creed

Redemption as the Second Key to an Evangelical Design

The truth is . . . that from the earliest time economics
was a theological issue, and it still is.
—Justo Gonzalez, *Faith and Wealth*

My original goal was to understand those early Christians in Philippi who worshipped within an octagonal building. My instincts told me that an emphasis on "the eighth day" would lead to a connection between Sunday and Monday. Furthermore, I wanted to delve into Luther's *Small Catechism* to see if Luther defined Christian discipleship by using the terminology of faith, work, and economics.

What we discover in the *Small Catechism* is that the first bridge between Sunday and Monday is the Ten Commandments. Luther used the first section of his catechism to reflect on God's law in relationship to all aspects of faith, work, and economics. The connections were strong and direct. I'm now shocked I didn't see these obvious references earlier in my ministry.

Now we move to the next section of the *Small Catechism* to see if these same themes continue as Luther teaches about the Holy Trinity. The key question is, Will Luther's explanation of the Holy Trinity also make a connection between Sunday and Monday? Can the Apostles' Creed effectively frame our daily work, or is it imprisoned in Sunday worship and theological garble? The second chapter of the catechetical story is the creed.

I never liked the Apostles' Creed as a young youth leader in the church. The creeds were simply too long, especially the Nicene Creed. I wondered why we confessed these creeds every Sunday. Was this necessary? Creedal language seemed odd and antiquated. When I spoke the words aloud by rote, I often traveled in my mind to faraway places. It was hard to focus. At no other time of the week did I use any of the three historic creeds of the church. They could have been labeled "For Sundays Only."

I didn't think much about the Apostles' Creed as a youth until one of my high school friends confronted me with her concern for my eternal salvation. She meant well. Her attack on my faith hurt nevertheless and left a mark on my soul. At her church, she had learned that "mainline Christians" weren't really Christian at all. Most evangelicals make distinctions among mainline Christians, or "liberals"—meaning, between those that may believe correctly and those that don't. Concerning Lutherans, this involves at least parsing the differences among the Wisconsin Synod (WS), Missouri Synod (MS), and Evangelical Lutheran Church in America (ELCA) Lutherans. One of the groups is usually labeled "liberal" by evangelicals and thus spiritually deficient. That "liberal" tag represents my Lutheran tribe today. In the 1970s, however, my congregation was in the Missouri Synod. The Missouri Synod is generally considered to be conservative and relatively orthodox among most evangelicals. I should have passed the "orthodox" test then, but my friend had obviously not learned the nuances yet in judging other Christians, and Lutherans in particular. Honestly, these labels are mostly inaccurate and harmful generalizations. Remember how the Eighth Commandment forbids bearing false witness?

My friend and I were in the high school choir together, so we got to know each other well. We even had time to share our religious beliefs. She concluded one day that because my church practiced a formal liturgy, and thus used creeds, my faith was merely intellectual in nature. She spoke openly about her fear for my salvation. She had certainly been taught this way of judging at her church. Because I used an ancient creed to confess my faith, I wasn't "born again."

I might even be going to hell. She hoped that I would come to her youth group and, more importantly, to a real heartfelt faith in Jesus, one that didn't use ancient words as an intellectual replacement for true faith.

Facing her "challenge" was the first time I had really thought seriously about those creeds. Unfortunately, I didn't have the resources, emotionally or theologically, to respond at that time. It did leave me with a spiritual bruise, though, and a fascination with those ancient creeds. Why had my friend so opposed them? They were boring, yes, but were they dangerous?

Luther's section on the Apostles' Creed might prove difficult for some evangelical Christians like my friend from high school, who belong to noncreedal church traditions. These churches affirm, "No creed but the Bible!" I understand these concerns. A creed can prove to be a good or a dangerous tool. But not having a creed can also prove dangerous. A person's faith can become susceptible to being blown around by every wind of doctrine or culture. Consequently, many "noncreedal" churches recognize the need to formulate some kind of "statement of faith" for their members. These statements almost always refer to God as Father, Son, and Holy Spirit, and emphasize the work of salvation through Christ. The authority of the Bible is defined. Some even mention a few specific laws that define orthodoxy, although these lists usually only mention laws about sex, abortion, and marriage.

I understand that these churches still want to encourage their members to read and prioritize the Bible. This is good. The Bible comes first before statements about the faith. Almost all church traditions affirm this point about the word of God. But many churches likewise feel the necessity of putting together a "confessional statement" so that a certain "orthodoxy" or a commitment to "correct biblical beliefs" prevails in the congregation. In writing down these "statements of faith," care is taken to remain true to central biblical pronouncements, focus in on the Triune God, and make sure that the person and work of Jesus as Savior and Lord remain central.

This is the goal of the Apostles' Creed. It's a statement of faith that tries to summarize biblical affirmations about God's activity in the world in a concise manner. The Apostles' Creed should not be approached primarily as *doctrine about* God. Rather, this creed tells a story about God in the form of a confession. More precisely, it's the second chapter of the story following the Ten Commandments. The commandments expose a massive problem. In response, the creed offers God's solution to that problem. This chapter of the story is organized around the Triune God's economic work in the world (i.e., the economic trinity): creation, redemption, and sanctification. Again, instead of theological statements per se, the creed is written as a story about God's activities in the world, much like the four Gospels. The Apostles' Creed is like a local congregation's "statement of faith" that has gone viral, accepted by generations of Christians around the world as an authoritative way to summarize and confess God's story. Finally—and this point is important—the Apostles' Creed is formulated as a gospel presentation to be confessed rather than merely a series of theological propositions for intellectual ascent. It's more than a statement of faith. The character of creed as faith formation and confession becomes clear in Luther's explanation of it. We are invited to enter and participate in this story. The God narrative quickly becomes personal and communal. This is a story that "I confess" or "we confess" to be most certainly true. Amen.

Whether one embraces creeds, statements of faith, or the Bible alone, my hope for this chapter is that the evangelical heart of the gospel will be affirmed and tested for its relationship to our three-part architectural designs of faith, work, and economics. In all the early catechisms, the goal of lifting up the Apostles' Creed was to understand the economic trinity, or God's economy. In particular, the story is about God as God's gift to humanity. That is the good news. In Christ, we get all of God as a free gift.

The next section will continue to use the format employed above. First, the article of the creed will be stated, then Luther's explanation, and finally, a commentary about each article's relationship to faith, work, and economics (FWE).

THE APOSTLES' CREED:
HOW TO TEACH ABOUT GOD AS GOOD NEWS

What is incredible about Luther's explanation of the Apostles' Creed's first article is how far he moves beyond the details of the Genesis story to explain creation in everyday economic terms. Creation becomes Luther's personal story. Genesis 1–3 looks at the six-day creation and covers familiar territory. God created the heavens and the earth out of chaos. The creation includes earth and sky, plants and animals, a garden and humanity, people both male and female. Instead of repeating the Genesis account, in contrast, Luther goes into much more detail about his own life. He gets very personal about his own relationship with God's creative activity every day.[1]

The First Article: On Creation

I believe in God, the Father almighty, creator of heaven and earth.

What is this? or *What does this mean?*
I believe that God has created me together with all that exists. God has given me and still preserves my body and soul: eyes, ears, and all limbs and senses; reason and all mental faculties.

   In addition, God daily and abundantly provides shoes and clothing, food and drink, house and farm, spouse and children, fields, livestock, and all property—along with all the necessities and nourishment for this body and life. God protects me against all danger and shields and preserves me from all evil. And all this is done out of pure, fatherly, and divine goodness and mercy, without any merit or worthiness of mine at all! For all of this I owe it to God to thank and praise, serve, and obey him. This is most certainly true.

FWE Commentary

This is a remarkably detailed list! And it's personal! The list is grounded more in Luther's own life than in details found in Genesis 1–3. For Luther, believing in the God of creation has massive personal and economic implications. Our whole being, body and soul, was crafted by God. Everything we experience in our economic lives from education to housing, from food to health care, from clothes to manufacturing, from jobs to good government, from family relationships to just courts of law, from banks to business, from police to schools—all that we experience in the economy—is interpreted by Luther under the rubric "all is a gift." God as creator gives good gifts so that people flourish. One is reminded of the petition of the Lord's Prayer where we ask God for "daily bread." Daily bread symbolizes all of God's gifts to us in the form of daily provisions. One of God's greatest gifts in creation is the whole, complex economy, which, as Luther proceeds, is there to provide all "necessities and nourishment for this body and life." "Daily bread" is thus a part of creation. Furthermore, as Creator, "God protects me against all danger and shields and preserves me from all evil." God's objective as Creator is to create and sustain the created world that God so loves.

Luther's notion of vocation also applies to this article of the Apostles' Creed. This idea harkens back to the Fourth Commandment. God has created work "in the garden" to provide and sustain humanity and all creation. These various vocations or callings are built by God into the created order for the purpose of serving the neighbor. God wants the neighbor to flourish. Creation and call happen together: "Vocation is always about service, not about self-care. Vocation counters the materialism and self-centeredness of economic pursuits by giving them a new meaning and a new orientation."[2] Loving the neighbor is the goal. Creation is received through service to others.

"If we believed," Luther writes referring to this article of the creed, "we would also act accordingly, and not swagger about and boast and brag as if we had life, riches, power, honor and such things of ourselves."[3] Thus, the essence of the church's ancient teaching of the economic trinity begins with creation as a gift. That is the first of God's activities in the world. God provides for our every need. That's God's economy at work. In response, we live lives of gratitude: "We thank, praise, serve, and obey God."

This article also comes with a burden—literally, a debt of gratitude to be paid. Luther uses the economic term *owe* or *debt*. Timothy Wengert explains the "debt" in the following way: "In the *Large Catechism*, we discover the exposition of this debt when Luther writes, in what must be surprising language for many today, 'This article would humble and terrify us all, if we believed it.'"[4]

Wengert goes on to explain,

> Humble? Terrify? How is this possible? Is not creation all about beautiful sunsets, human beings made in God's image with infinite possibilities, babies nestling in their mothers' arms—and a whiff of apple pie in the kitchen? Not for Luther. The first article—that we live in a created world that comes to us as a sheer gift from God and that we ourselves are creatures, not creators—comes with an enormous burden. If all that is around us and in us is good, bestowed by a good God and received as a sheer gift, then we are in trouble—given what we actually do with creation. In the *Large Catechism*, Luther began with our own limbs—the gifts of our arms and legs, mouths, brains, eyes, ears—and looked at how we use them against our neighbor, sometimes even against our very selves! Then, if one considers the other gifts of creation—air, water, earth, fire (to name the four elements Luther knew about)—where do we stand? If one could somehow survive Luther's exposition of the Ten Commandments and remain sinless, this article would finally put the lie to our rebellious, self-centered ways. This article *would* humble and terrify us.[5]

This article on creation leaves any believer in a bad economic state—that is, in debt to God. Our debt revolves around our lack of gratitude to God for all God's gifts to us. The gifts are everywhere. Yet we pretend that we've earned it all, accomplished it all, built it all. Our accomplishments in the economy become primary. Look at how we have pulled ourselves up by our bootstraps. God is pushed to the background, if God's in the picture at all. Life is no longer a gift.

Praise shrivels up in this narcissistic situation, and prayer becomes dry like a desert. Our debt of gratitude grows.

The second article of the Apostles' Creed will deal with our "debt problem" through another act of God. God's economy expands.

The Second Article: On Redemption

I believe in Jesus Christ, God's only son, our Lord, who was conceived by the Holy Spirit, born of the virgin Mary, suffered under Pontius Pilate, was crucified, died, and was buried; he descended to the dead. On the third day he rose again; he ascended into heaven, he is seated at the right hand of the Father, and he will come to judge the living and the dead.

What is this? or *What does this mean?*
I believe that Jesus Christ, true God, begotten of the Father in eternity, and also a true human being, born of the virgin Mary, is my Lord. He has redeemed me, a lost and condemned human being. He has purchased and freed me from all sins, from death, and from the power of the devil, not with gold or silver but with his holy, precious blood and his innocent suffering and death. He has done all this in order that I may belong to him, live under him in his kingdom, and serve him in eternal righteousness, innocence, and blessedness, just as he is risen from the dead and lives and rules eternally. This is most certainly true.

FWE Commentary
The key to the second article of the Apostles' Creed for Luther was the phrase "our Lord." He writes, "If you are asked, What do you mean when you say, 'I believe in Jesus Christ . . .' respond: 'This is what I mean by saying this, that Jesus Christ true Son of God has been made my Lord.'"[6]

Luther goes on to describe that Jesus could only be Lord because of his role as Redeemer. It is fascinating that Luther highlights an economic term at this point:

I ought to believe and do believe that Christ is my Lord, that is, that he redeemed me, because the second article [of the Apostles' Creed] talks about this. He defeats death and sin and frees me from them. First, when I was created, I had all kinds of blessings (the body, etc.), but I served sin, death, etc. Then Christ came, who suffered death so that I might be freed from death and become his son and be led into righteousness, life, etc. "Lord" means the same as "Redeemer" etc. The other sections [of this article] show how he set up the whole thing and what price he paid: not with gold, silver or equities [nor with arms, swords, and human powers] but with himself, that is, with his own body [and blood].[7]

Wengert points out that in Luther's day, "people would have expected that lords were responsible to protect their subjects and, should it happen, rescue them from false imprisonment or kidnapping."[8] Redemption, therefore, was a doctrine of salvation taught to the good people of Wittenberg in a way that corresponded to their daily experiences. Speculative philosophies were of no concern here: "Kidnapping for ransom was not an unknown occupation in early modern Germany."[9] This was much more graspable than Anselm's theories of vicarious satisfaction, where God pays "someone" to free sinners through Christ's suffering and death.[10]

Luther knew this "redemption tradition." Everyone understood the role of a lord was to redeem—that is, to pay ransom and win back his subjects. It's this tradition that informs how Luther explains this second article of the creed concerning Jesus's role as Lord. Luther is not explaining a philosophical theory concerning the doctrine of redemption. He is explaining his experience of liberation from those forces around him that want to keep him in captivity: the world, sin, death, and the devil. "Our Lord," then for Luther, means that Jesus pays the ransom for one of his own. I now belong to Jesus. He has purchased me. Jesus is my Lord.

The Third Article: On Life in the Kingdom

I believe in the Holy Spirit, the holy catholic church, the communion of saints, the forgiveness of sins, the resurrection of the body, and the life everlasting. Amen.

What is this? or *What does this mean?*
I believe that by my own understanding or strength I cannot believe in Jesus Christ my Lord or come to him, but instead the Holy Spirit has called me through the gospel, enlightened me with his gifts, made me holy and kept me in the true faith, just as he calls, gathers, enlightens, and makes holy the whole Christian church on earth and keeps it with Jesus Christ in the one common, true faith. Daily in this Christian church the Holy Spirit abundantly forgives all sins—mine and those of all believers. On the last day the Holy Spirit will raise me and all the dead and will give to me and all believers in Christ eternal life. This is most certainly true.

FWE Commentary
Here the emphasis is on the kingdom of God. The Lordship of Jesus represents a new kind of management or stewardship of the world. Paul calls it a new "dispensation." This kingdom is moved, filled, and directed by the Holy Spirit. Any language used to describe the Lordship of Jesus over our lives vis-à-vis faith, work, and economics must be marinated in Holy Spirit talk. That is the point of the catechism's structure: Creation leads to redemption. Redemption opens the possibility of living within Jesus's Lordship through the Holy Spirit. "God's kingdom" can be described as "God's economy." The Holy Spirit works within this kingdom or economy therefore in freedom: "For freedom Christ has set us free" (Gal 5:1). The kingdom of God is not a "rule-by-law" kind of existence. This kingdom or economy is a rule-by-the-Spirit operation. This Spirit is a gift, our inheritance. Life in this economy is not governed by a virtue achieved by hard work, character curriculums, or disciplined action. As "good" as these efforts may be, and as wonderful these fruits may taste, they don't

represent the kingdom of God described in the third article. God's kingdom is gifted to us by the Spirit and always received and exercised through faith. This happens not by hard work or workshops on character formation. Faith, work, and economic language must always be grounded in this faith dynamic of the Spirit's work in the believer when speaking of life within God's economy. Otherwise, law reigns rather than faith. The eighth day of creation is thus a new day generated by the Holy Spirit.

EVANGELISM AND THE CREED

D. James Kennedy developed a popular evangelism program in the 1970s and '80s called Evangelism Explosion.[11] This program was used extensively in Lutheran congregations at that time, including my Lutheran congregation in Dayton, Ohio, Emmanuel Lutheran Church. My father taught this conversational approach to evangelism with great conviction and excitement. The classes were a big success. At first, however, few people signed up for the courses. So Dad did what any pastor with a large family would do in this situation: he signed up his sons to get the program started. As a result, my brothers and I learned to share the faith in people's homes.

The program was designed to move a gospel presentation from big stadiums, like with Billy Graham, to small living rooms. The assumption was that people would be more open to a conversation about their faith in the comfort of their own homes. The conversation started by asking two diagnostic questions as spiritual icebreakers:

1. Have you come to a place in your spiritual life where you *know for certain* that if you were to die tonight you would go to heaven?
2. Suppose that you were to die tonight and stand before God and he were to say to you, "Why should I let you into my heaven?" What would you say?[12]

The answers to both questions—not only for unbelievers but for churchgoers of all stripes!—were shocking. Many had gone to church their whole lives. They had attended Bible studies. So it was a surprise that their answers to these two questions were often the same as those who had never gone to church before. "I'm not sure" was usually the answer to the first question. They had no assurance of God's love in Christ. In response to the second question, the answer was worse: "I'm not perfect but I hope I've done enough. I've tried to live a good life." In other words, they weren't sure they had done enough to earn heaven as a reward. Notice the emphasis on their own actions.

The sixteenth-century Reformation opposed this approach to God. The religion of "I've tried to live enough of a good life to earn God's favor" was the religious posture Luther was trying to destroy with his evangelical catechism. These were the same answers he confronted on his parish visitations. He opposed these attitudes toward God because they didn't correspond to the scriptural proclamation of the good news in Christ, and ultimately, they were destructive to a person's relationship with God. When do any of us know if we have done enough to please God?

One powerful way to protest against this attitude of earning God's favor was to change the order of the catechism. Changing the order of the catechism also changed the way the gospel was presented to people as good news. For Luther, this reordering of the catechism, beginning with the commandments instead of the Apostles' Creed, was one of the keys to his evangelical renewal. Wengert describes the rearrangement of the order in this way: "The [old] order was the order of *musts*—from Creed to commandments to prayer. Here is what you must believe; now that you believe, here's what you must do; now that you feel guilty, here are the right words to pray. The new order was the order of baptism: from death to resurrection, from terror to faith and comfort; from commandments to Creed, that is, from law to gospel."[13]

Luther himself described the new order of the catechism in this way:

Three things people must know in order to be saved. First, they must know what to do and what to leave undone. Second, when they realize that they cannot measure up to what they should do or leave undone, they need to know where to go to find the strength they require. Third, they must know how to seek and obtain that strength. It is just like a sick person who first must determine the nature of his sickness, then find out what to do or to leave undone. After that he must know where to get the medicine which will help him do or leave undone what is right for a healthy person. Third, he has to desire to search for this medicine and to obtain it or have it brought to him. Thus, the commandments teach humans to begin to recognize their sickness. . . . The Creed will teach and show them where to find the medicine—grace—which will help them to become devout and keep the commandments. The Creed points them to God and his mercy, given and made plain to them in Christ. Finally, the Lord's Prayer teaches all this, namely, through the fulfillment of God's commandment [by faith] everything will be given to them.[14]

The order of the catechism may seem too minuscule an issue for many at this juncture, like theological hairsplitting with no obvious purpose. The opposite is true. The order of the catechetical material is underlined here because in our attempts at connecting Sunday with Monday, it will be easy to lose the reality of "faith in Christ." If "faith" disappears, only the "to dos" or "musts" of the commandments remain. Faith then is degraded and becomes merely an inspirational tool for doing God's law. Christ's work of the cross becomes *only* a spiritual force and/or motivation for performing the law in the marketplace, work, or school. Death and resurrection play no daily role here. There's no new creation. No freedom. Just the status quo now emboldened by Jesus. All we get on Sundays is the power to accomplish the old laws through Jesus, not freedom to move into anything new by faith.

The consequence for today's conversations around faith, work, and economics couldn't be weightier. Will the main connection between Sunday and Monday be primarily "ethical," a series of "musts" that

Christians take with them into the home and marketplace? Or is there something about faith itself that preserves and transforms the marketplace? The family? Our neighborhoods? Is our goal to teach virtue and character to improve the first creation, or is it to promote a faith in Christ that can navigate and transform daily life into something new? Commandments cannot transform life. Not even good ones! Commandments can't lead us to "new creation." Commandments regulate and guide our lives. Period. Faith, as proclaimed in Scripture, is what promotes Christian living within the eighth day of creation. Faith functions without law (Gal 3). It's entrepreneurial. It acts out of freedom. Life expressed within Christian freedom is at the heart of eighth-day discipleship.

Let's be clear: Christian freedom is often misunderstood. Even by Christians. Especially Christian leaders! It always has been. Warning, warning, the flock is free! The letter to the Galatians testifies to this fear even among the earliest believers. Some argued that faith in Christ meant going back to obey the Jewish law or another set of laws. Being part of God's kingdom and part of God's chosen people was based on following the law. The call to Christian freedom, however, is not a call to follow the law; it is the call to faith in Christ: "For freedom Christ has set us free" (Gal 5:1). Eighth-day Christians embrace this freedom in faith and don't return to a life driven by dos and don'ts. The life of freedom in God's kingdom economy is what we are called to explore. The law leads to death. Faith leads to resurrection and life. The catechism helps us figure out this tricky dynamic. Above all, as the gospel teaches us that before the new is given, the old must die—daily.

Why is this distinction important? Let me suggest two reasons. First, the way one disciples a Christian can promote either a law-oriented or faith-oriented life. Some Protestants today, unfortunately, agree with the old pre-Reformation emphasis on the role of God's law in daily life: "The tradition, still dominant today, interprets God's calling in terms of demands upon Jesus' followers, as an application of the moral law."[15] God's grace through Christ, in this model, simply empowers believers to go back and follow the commandments, but now with the power of Jesus behind them. Jesus becomes more of a parole officer than a liberator. Luther's catechism critiques this model as insufficient, even as disobedient. Eighth-day faith is not possible if our whole life is about following commandments. This distinction lies at the heart of the Reformation's insight into the gospel of Jesus Christ.

Second, all ancient catechisms used the same three pillars of the faith to teach discipleship: the Ten Commandments, the Apostles' Creed, and the Lord's Prayer. This simple insight is instructive because these three pillars are rarely used in today's discussions about faith, work, and economics. Protestants tend to use specific texts from the Bible and apply biblical principles for daily life. Others may emphasize theologies of creation and justice. These tools are fine, of course, in their place. But if the Ten Commandments summarize God's law, why not explore and teach this tool for use in daily life? And if the Apostles' Creed summarizes the faith in the Triune God's activity in the world, then why not explore and use this tool for daily life? Finally, if the Lord's Prayer is Jesus's own summary of how we should pray for the kingdom, then this prayer should certainly be a powerful tool for bridging the gap between Sunday and Monday.

The three initial pillars of the *Small Catechism* provide ample resources for any eight-sided church. Experiencing the catechism's structure is like walking a person through a well-designed cathedral. The architecture affects you. In theological parlance, we call this design "the order of salvation." It's a gospel presentation that is ordered or designed to affect a person living inside it along the lines of the word of God. The design is this:

Commandments lead to a need for . . .
redemption. Redemption leads to . . .
prayer for the kingdom.

This movement is the evangelical three-step. Life that is first ordered by commandments ends up being transformed and freed up by Christ for life within God's kingdom and God's economy. The third movement of this divine design is the Lord's Prayer, a prayer for the kingdom. This kingdom is not one built with laws. It's not a kingdom characterized by rules and regulations. It's also not an economy ordered with principles on stone tablets. The Lord's Prayer describes this economy and kingdom very differently, as we will see in the next chapter.

CONCLUSION

The Apostles' Creed as laid out in the *Small Catechism* connects Sunday with Monday in every article. Thus, the creed should not be imprisoned on Sunday mornings. It's useful for our daily lives. Creation describes the gifts that we have received from our Creator in terms of all our daily possessions, including our family, work, and economic well-being. These are all gifts from God, which creates a debt of gratitude. Unfortunately, this debt of gratitude is never paid entirely because we have other lords in our lives, including our own efforts at self-rule. Our work reigns supreme. The economy drives our life. The market calls the shots. Many lords vie for control of our life and demand loyalty. Above all else, we want to be in charge. We think we're independent. Idolatry runs rampant, not gratitude.

This is why we need a Lord who can "redeem" us from these other lords, purchasing us with a holy price. After claiming us as his own, Jesus grants us a final gift, the Holy Spirit, the gift that guides the Christian through faith in all matters of faith, work, and economic activity. This gift connects Sunday and Monday in a new way. This is a gift that leads to and thrives in the responsibility and freedom of the eighth day of creation.

6

The Catechism and the Lord's Prayer

The Kingdom of God as the Third Key to an Evangelical Design

> What did Jesus Christ add to Athens and Rome that
> altered the human conception of political economy?
> —Michael Novak, *How Christianity Changed
> Political Economy*

We turn now to the prayer for God's kingdom, which, as the third chapter of the evangelical story, promotes God's economy in Christ. The Lord's Prayer is the third step in the evangelical dance. Notice two insights right from the start. First, whereas the Ten Commandments and the Apostles' Creed speak more to the individual ("*I* believe"), the Lord's Prayer speaks from the position of the community. "*Our* Father" is how we address God, not "*my* Father." The emphasis is on community because that is what faith and the kingdom do: they create community. The Lord's Prayer represents a conversion from individualism and self-interest to community.

Second, the Lord's Prayer maps out life in the kingdom without laws. We might instinctively think that this prayer from Jesus would give us laws to protect us against specific dangers in the world. That it might be like another tablet from Moses, filled with rules and regulations. Or maybe we expect a system of piety teachings that help us avoid certain "temptations" and "trials." Three "counsels" were practiced at the time of Luther and still are today by people who are really committed to the deeper spiritual life. These counsels or vows commit a disciple to a life of poverty, chastity, and obedience. So we look at the Lord's Prayer and ask: Does this prayer teach us to avoid economic issues, money, and daily needs? As we discover in the *Small Catechism*, the opposite is the case. The prayer teaches us how to live in the kingdom while living in the world. Kingdom and world belong together. The prayer encourages a commitment to God's economy in the world. Or, as Jesus says to his disciples, to be "in" the world, but not "of" it (John 17:14–16).

THE GREAT MARTYR OF THE CHURCH

Luther is often quoted as saying that the Lord's Prayer is the greatest martyr on earth.[1] The reason behind this sad commentary is that we kill the prayer every time we say it without thought or focus. In other words, all the time!

In high school, our football team assembled in the end zone before every game and said the Lord's Prayer. All fifty players! Christian and non-Christian alike, these fighting football Chiefs prayed Jesus's prayer for the kingdom. Everyone seemed to know it by heart. But did they? I don't know. I had my eyes shut. The same held true for the basketball team in our public school. We prayed the Lord's Prayer in the locker room. Only the baseball team skipped the prayer altogether. Why did the coaches have us say this prayer before every game? Was it an issue of faith? Was it superstition? Or was it to motivate our players spiritually before we "killed the other team"? Maybe it was done because that's what teams were supposed to do—at least in the 1970s.

What I find strange is that we athletes said that prayer religiously before games at school on Friday nights but not so much at the church during youth meetings. Odd. Our youth group prayed before every meeting, but we never used the Lord's Prayer. Never. The Lord's Prayer at church was exclusively prayed in worship on Sundays and at formal church council meetings. The church's council meeting would always close with the Lord's Prayer. This was the tradition. And spontaneity in prayer was feared. Again, the question still haunts me. Why did athletes want to pray that prayer before every game, but our church youth group didn't? Why did I never pray this prayer privately or at home?

TWO LORD'S PRAYERS

There are two renderings of the Lord's Prayer in the Bible. The first one is embedded in Jesus's Sermon on the Mount, in Matthew 6:9–13. This is the version most often memorized by Christians, used in worship services, employed in public gatherings, and even prayed at sporting events. Matthew's version was the one our high school football team used before every game. Who knew! And we prayed it in King James's English too (e.g., "Hallowed be thy name")!

Matthew's version of the Lord's Prayer is the version used in the *Small Catechism*. This version will be the basis of our commentary and discussion below.

A second version of the Lord's Prayer is the shorter rendition, in Luke 11:2–4. Only five petitions are listed in Luke. I mention Luke's version briefly for two reasons. First, it's easier to see "work" and "economic" references when only five petitions are listed. The petitions about "daily bread" and "forgiveness of sin/debts" are obvious. And second, Luke uses different language around "forgiveness" than Matthew. Luke uses both economic and noneconomic language for sin in the same petition.

Matthew uses the word *debt* twice in this petition: "Forgive us our debts as we forgive our debtors." Luke, in contrast, uses "sin" and "debt." The term *trespasses* is not used by either in the prayer itself. Although they use different language, Matthew and Luke point to forgiveness in ways that are both monetary (debts) and nonmonetary (sins). One could then argue that praying for the kingdom, as defined by Jesus, includes work-related and economic terms. These economic references might be overlooked if you use the language of "trespasses" in the Lord's Prayer, as I was taught as a child. It makes sense that a prayer for God's economy (God's kingdom) would employ economic terms.[2]

Luke version of Jesus's prayer reads:

Father, hallowed be your name.
Your kingdom come.
Give us each day our daily bread.
And forgive us our sins,
　　for we ourselves forgive everyone indebted to us.
And do not bring us to the time of trial. (Luke 11:2–4)

In Luther's catechism, the language of "forgiveness" reflects faithfully the monetary and nonmonetary references in both Matthew and Luke—that is, "sins" and "debts." The economic implications here surrounding forgiveness are often lost in worship. Luther understood that Jesus was referring here to Deuteronomy 15 and the Sabbath laws of debt forgiveness. It's fascinating that the church writings, from ancient times through the Reformation, make this same connection. Forgiveness in the Lord's Prayer involves both interpersonal issues (guilt and shame) and monetary issues (loans and debts). Relationships with our neighbor involve both. Forgiveness therefore deals with both.

The key to understanding this prayer for the kingdom is that it is all about God's stewardship or management of the community, the big picture of God's governance of all things. Any time Jesus talks about the "kingdom," he is talking about God's economy. Using the same format found elsewhere, we'll follow Luther through the prayer, one petition at a time. Afterward, a commentary on faith, work, and economics (FWE) will be provided.[3]

THE LORD'S PRAYER:
HOW TO PRAY FOR THE KINGDOM OF GOD
Introduction

Our Father in heaven.

What is this? or *What does this mean?*
With these words God wants to attract us, so that we come to believe he is truly our Father and we are truly his children, in order that we

may ask him boldly and with complete confidence, just as loving children ask their loving Father.

FWE Commentary
The language here is liberating. We are to approach our heavenly parent for all needs, just like a child comes to a parent. No request is out of bounds, including daily items involving our families, work, economic challenges, and vocational discernment. We also say this prayer as a community, a group, a body. We recognize that God isn't just "my" or "my group's" Father. Tribalism is not an option. The prayer in faith recognizes that we aren't alone in the kingdom. God has placed us together with others in Christ. That's what faith does. The implication of the *our* for our work and economic lives is enormous. We are no longer individuals engaged in a materialistic game, trapped in the prison of self-interest. God frees us from that life of *homo economicus* and the prosperity gospel and unites us to others in a life of love and service. When we are united with others, triumphant tribalism is eliminated, and personal happiness is no longer our life's goal.

The mention of heaven also reminds us that God through Christ is ruling the world. Jesus is Lord! The Father put the Son at his right hand on the throne of grace. We are called to participate in God's economy. God is the steward and the manager. The world as a garden belongs to God. So too does the New Jerusalem.

The First Petition

Hallowed be your name.

What is this? or *What does this mean?*
It is true that God's name is holy in itself, but we ask in this prayer that it may also become holy in and among us.

How does this come about?
Whenever the word of God is taught clearly and purely and we, as God's children, also live holy lives according to it. To this end help us,

dear Father in heaven! However, whoever teaches and lives otherwise than the word of God teaches, dishonors the name of God among us. Preserve us from this, heavenly Father!

FWE Commentary
The use of the unfamiliar word *hallowed* is quite fascinating. Luther correlates it with "keeping holy," thus living by faith. He writes in the catechism "that God's name is holy in itself." This language underlines the message that God is holy, righteous, and faithful. N. T. Wright claims that this language emerges from the Exodus narrative where God "hallows" God's name by bringing the chosen people through the wilderness into the promised land.[4] God hallows God's name consequently by saving Israel from slavery. God hallows God's name when God fulfills promises by providing Abraham with children as numerous as the stars (Gen 15:5–6). God hallows God's name when the exiles in Babylon are returned to Jerusalem. So when we say this prayer, we want to keep God's name holy. We want to teach and keep the word of God pure. More importantly, however, we pray in faith, believing God will fulfill God's promises to us. This petition is like a confession. God is faithful. Amen! We affirm in faith that God will be faithful to us in Christ in all aspects of our lives. Therefore, we confess in this prayer our confidence in God's promise, that God's name is holy in itself. God can fulfill what God has promised to us vis-à-vis our whole life, including our work and our economy.

The Second Petition
Your kingdom come.

What is this? or *What does this mean?*
In fact, God's kingdom comes on its own without our prayer, but we ask in this prayer that it may also come to us.

How does this come about?
Whenever our heavenly Father gives us his Holy Spirit, so that through the Holy Spirit's grace we believe God's holy word and live godly lives here in time and hereafter in eternity.

FWE Commentary
This petition takes us back to the third article of the Apostles' Creed. We know that the kingdom of God is linked with the gift of the Holy Spirit. God's economy is not about following laws but about following the Spirit in faith. Freedom and faith go together. All benefits that come through the Holy Spirit come through faith exercised in freedom. The implications for a transformation for our work and economic lives are massive. If we are to move from an economic engagement with the world run by laws—even good, divinely inspired laws—to an engagement run by the Holy Spirit, faith will be necessary. That is at the heart of this petition. If our goal at work is to merely be virtuous, that is praiseworthy, but it's not the kingdom. If our goal at school is to act out of a good character, that is also praiseworthy, but it's not necessarily life in the kingdom. Good character and virtue are not automatically to be understood as the fruits of faith. Faith is more. Faith in Christ will lead us to a life of freedom that opens the possibility of a new life in Christ and the work of new creation. Living in the kingdom is living in the eternal eighth day of creation. Doing the old and new work simultaneously is what was meant by living ambidextrously: in faith, obeying laws to help care for the first creation while also in freedom creating the new.

The Third Petition

Your will be done, on earth as in heaven.

What is this? or *What does this mean?*
In fact, God's good and gracious will comes about without our prayer, but we ask in this prayer that it may also come about in and among us.

How does this come about?
Whenever God breaks and hinders every evil scheme and will—as are present in the will of the devil, the world, and our flesh—that would not allow us to hallow God's name and would prevent the coming of his kingdom, and instead whenever God strengthens us and keeps us steadfast in his word and in faith until the end of our lives. This is God's gracious and good will.

FWE Commentary
What might get in the way of Jesus's Lordship over our lives? The enemies are listed here: sin, the world, the devil, and our flesh. These same enemies will prevent us from living out our work and our economic lives in ways that please God. Each one presents a different threat. These enemies want to prevent the word of God from creating faith in us so that we abandon God's kingdom. The eighth day is the enemy of all sin and evil forces. Living our lives "in faith" fulfills this petition—that is, to do God's will on earth as it is in heaven. In the kingdom, God's will is done through faith and trust, not through law keeping. God demands to be Lord over every aspect of our lives, including our families, our work, the public square, and our religious community. Our prayer here is to have the kingdom and God's economy penetrate every aspect of our lives.

When we are living in the kingdom by faith, we are confident that God is loving the world through us. God is governing through us. God is stewarding through us. God's economy is now taking hold in our neighborhoods through us. God's work, our hands.

The Fourth Petition

Give us today our daily bread.

What is this? or *What does this mean?*
In fact, God gives daily bread without our prayer, even to all evil people, but we ask in this prayer that God causes us to recognize what our daily bread is and to receive it with thanksgiving.

What then does "daily bread" mean?
Everything included in the necessities and nourishment for our bodies, such as food, drink, clothing, shoes, house, farm, fields, livestock, money, property, an upright spouse, upright children, upright members of the household, upright and faithful rulers, good government, good weather, peace, health, decency, honor, good friends, faithful neighbors, and the like.

FWE Commentary
This petition directly references our work and our economic lives. The list of personal and economic factors is not exhaustive here, but it is comprehensive. This petition points to the first article of the Apostles' Creed, but now we recognize that these gifts are all a part of God's kingdom. Faith gives us eyes to see creation in a new way. In God's economy, our daily needs are met. We are content. Faith in Christ teaches us this. So too are our neighbors' needs met, for we pray as a community: "Give *us* today our daily bread." Jesus's prayer makes direct reference to God's provision of manna for the children of Israel in the wilderness (Exod 11). The manna was good for only one day. Storehouses of manna were not possible. This petition uses this wilderness story to teach about the kingdom. Daily trust in God to meet our daily needs is the result of faith. As Gene Veith explains,

> When we pray the Lord's Prayer, to use one of Luther's illustrations, we ask God to give us this day our daily bread. And God does. The way God gives us our daily bread is *through* the vocations of farmers, millers, and bakers. In our modern economy, we might add truck drivers, factory workers, bankers, warehouse attendants, and food service workers. Virtually every facet of our whole economic system contributes to that piece of toast we just enjoyed for breakfast. Now add jelly and a few pieces of bacon and the list of participants in your "daily bread" grows exponentially. When we thank God for our food before we eat, we are right to do so. God does

provide our food, and God does so by means of vocations; that is, by means of ordinary people just doing their jobs.[5]

Every job now becomes essential work.

Consequently, this petition encourages us to serve our neighbor in ways that provide them their daily bread. The power of this petition in any neighborhood is vast. You can't pray this prayer and not start feeding the poor, clothing the naked, or healing the sick. Engagement in the community deepens when we pray for daily bread in God's economy.

The Fifth Petition

Forgive us our sins [debts] as we forgive those who sin against us [as we also have forgiven our debtors].

What is this? or *What does this mean?*
We ask in this prayer that our heavenly Father would not regard our sins nor deny these petitions on their account, for we are worthy of nothing for which we ask, nor have we earned it. Instead, we ask that God would give us all things by grace, for we sin daily and indeed deserve only punishment. So, on the other hand, we, too, truly want to forgive heartily and to do good gladly to those who sin against us.

FWE Commentary
Luther follows the biblical language with this petition, not choosing the word often used in the English-speaking world: trespasses. Forgiveness is thus linked to financial matters. The sabbatical laws of Deuteronomy 15 are the direct reference. Our neighbors are never to suffer too long under the weight of debt or the loss of their means for a sustainable life (e.g., their land or a job). In the seventh year of the debt, in Deuteronomy, the debt was to be forgiven. The reason for this debt forgiveness was to maintain the health of the community. (Interestingly, these sabbatical laws didn't apply to foreign loans.) In reference to these laws, Jesus asks us to forgive debts in the

same manner as we have forgiven our debtors. The financial references are so strong that Matthew adds another section after this prayer to include the notion of nonmonetary "sin" (Matt 6:14–15). In other words, Matthew makes additions so that we don't just limit this commandment to economic issues. Matthew now adds the word *trespasses* to make the point: "For if you forgive others their trespasses, your heavenly Father will also forgive you; but if you do not forgive others, neither will your Father forgive your trespasses" (Matt 6:16–17).

Luke's Gospel combines the language of "sin" and "debts," as mentioned above (see Luke 11:4). Even with a different language being used, the emphasis is clear: our relationships to God and neighbor are intertwined. So too are the financial and interpersonal dimensions of relationships intertwined. We get this. Love of God and love of neighbor cannot avoid the issues of money and debt. Economic issues are always tied to forgiveness because financial issues are tied together with most of our relationships in the family and community. When forgiveness is needed, economic issues are never far away.

The Sixth Petition

Save us from the time of trial.

What is this? or *What does this mean?*

It is true that God tempts no one, but we ask in this prayer that God would preserve and keep us, so that the devil, the world, and our flesh may not deceive us or mislead us into false belief, despair, and other great and shameful sins, and that, although we may be attacked by them, we may finally prevail and gain the victory.

FWE Commentary

What temptation might be so impactful and devastating that it could ruin our faith? Many issues might be listed here, including bad behavior by Christians and outright hypocrisy by the church. Many evils exist in the world that might cause this deep level of doubt and despair. These evils include economic issues such as poverty, disease, illness, hunger, and the shattered lives that economic injustice creates. Losing one's work or employment can create an existential crisis of financial want, of course, but it can also affect one's identity and purpose in life. Our prayer is that God saves us from these trials and their consequences. This prayer also touches our neighbor. We don't want our neighbor to experience these trials and have their faith negatively impacted either. This petition leads to social engagement with the neighbor, for we know how devastating these trials and temptations can be.

The Seventh Petition

And deliver us from evil.

What is this? or *What does this mean?*
We ask in this prayer, as in a summary, that our Father in heaven may deliver us from all kinds of evil—affecting body or soul, property, or reputation—and at last, when our final hour comes, may grant us a blessed end, and take us by grace from this valley of tears to himself in heaven.

FWE Commentary
Certain evils can significantly undermine faith, even destroy it. Economic trials are at the top of this list of evils, alongside physical illnesses and family crises. "Evil" arises when dysfunctional systems or systemic injustices come into play—what the Bible sometimes calls "principalities and powers" (Eph 6:12; Col 1:16). War and pestilence often come to mind. Pandemics too. One should also include job loss, systemic racism, bias attached to sexual orientation, lack of creation care, and gender inequities. The list is endless, and nearly all these evils have economic ramifications. They can destroy our work, our employment, our reputations, our well-being, and unfortunately, our faith. These are important matters, so important that we pray that we, nor our neighbors, would not lose the kingdom and/or its blessings through these kinds of evil forces.

Conclusion

For the kingdom, the power, and the glory are yours, now and forever. Amen.

What is this? or *What does this mean?*
That I should be certain that such petitions are acceptable to and heard by our Father in heaven, for he himself commanded us to pray like this and has promised to hear us. "Amen, amen" means "Yes, yes, it is going to come about just like this."

FWE Commentary
We daily experience the impact of political, military, social, and economic powers. At the same time, eighth-day disciples, by the faith granted us by the Holy Spirit, recognize that Jesus is Lord, and he sits on the throne at the right hand of the Father. This is important to remember, especially on Monday! This Lord gives us permission to approach God in prayer confidently as Father. All power and glory belong to him. This is an integral dimension of the kingdom of God. The Holy Spirit teaches us who Jesus is and what benefits he puts at our disposal as his children living within the story of the eighth day of creation in God's good economy.

SUMMARY

How do we live as Christians within the resurrection tradition of the eighth day? How do we live by faith? How do we live as an eight-sided church in God's economy?

When I started writing this book, I wanted to return to my Reformation tradition to uncover any insight it might have into how to connect Sunday with Monday and faith with daily life. The modern conversation around faith, work, and economics was my catalyst. These categories were like architectural designs for building what I later discovered was an eight-sided church. Focusing on these categories helped me grasp life within the eighth day of creation. What

I found in the *Small Catechism*, to my amazement, was a treasure chest of resources. In fact, the resources were so numerous because the *Small Catechism* was written specifically for this purpose. This is evident already in its first three sections: the Ten Commandments, the Apostles' Creed, and the Lord's Prayer. That was not how I had received these catechetical pillars as a young adult on Saturday mornings when I painstakingly memorized their content word for word. That is because I learned the catechism when "work" and "economics" played little or no role in my life. Even as a seminarian and pastor, I don't remember the catechism's teachings applying to daily life in such direct ways. I didn't even use them this way as a professor of mission. More to the point, as a pastor, I didn't use the catechism to connect faith with work and economics. Now I wonder about the implications of not using these catechetical tools in reference to people's daily lives. Might the connection between Sunday and Monday be hampered when a person or community doesn't use these three fundamental pillars of the faith? The answer is a resounding yes.

My goals at the beginning of chapters 4, 5, and 6 were to discover whether the Reformation tradition expressed in Luther's *Small Catechism* could help me with my challenges, namely,

- the divorce between Sunday and Monday,
- the challenge of connecting faith with work and economic life, and
- how to become an eighth-day disciple.

What I discovered is that Luther's *Small Catechism* was written specifically to address the challenge of connecting Sunday and Monday in an evangelical way. It's not that the Reformation tradition had specific insights or principles to be gleaned for use in modern life. Rather the Reformation had produced a box of discipleship tools to accomplish, for Christians of all times and places, the very task of eighth-day discipleship for Monday.

Reformation scholars confirm the same message. Here is a sampling of what some scholars have said about how the *Small Catechism* was written to inform and form our daily lives along the lines of faith, work, and economics:

> This revolution [the connection among faith, daily life, and calling], which has often been completely lost in the Lutheran Church of the 21st century, comes to expression nowhere more clearly in Luther's writings than in the catechisms. Luther had discovered that justification was nothing less than the promise of a coming world. That world comes only through the gospel promise received by faith alone. . . . Instead of separating believers from the earthly realm, the Christian message revealed for Luther that the God and Father of Jesus is also Creator, and that Jesus is the one through whom all things are made. Thus, daily life is sanctified by faith alone. Rather than trying to escape this world or imagining that this world is all that there is, the Christian finds in the world God's call to love the neighbor.[6]

Martin Luther's Catechisms, both in what they critique and in what they encourage, promoted across very different contexts economic behaviors, anticipate what Nobel Laureate Muhammad Yunus first called "social businesses," or what have been dubbed, more broadly, "social enterprises."[7]

Although some scholars have described Luther as the first political economist, Luther understood himself as a pastor and theologian, radicalized by his grasp of justification by faith alone.[8]

Luther transformed this concept of the "calling" of believers or "vocation" by assigning it to all Christians. Believers recognize that God has placed them in the structures of human life created by God and has called them to the tasks of caring for other creatures, human and otherwise, as agents of God's providential presence and care. Luther called people in the exercise of their response-abilities "masks of God" through whom

God, for example, milks cows so that his human creature can be nourished. . . . He made this concept of callings of believers a basic element in his Small Catechism.[9]

Martin Luther is the great theologian of vocation. . . . To be sure, other theologians, such as Calvin and the Puritans, have taken Luther's doctrine of vocation in directions of their own. But it is in Luther's distinctive approach to vocation that the connections between faith, work, and economics emerge most clearly.[10]

Discovering the close relationship between faith, work, and economics has now become for me a catalyst for the rediscovery of my own Reformation tradition. More importantly, it is a rediscovery of the word of God. I couldn't see the centrality of these themes for years. Economic biases covered my eyes so that I couldn't see the obvious in the Bible and in my own church tradition. To my surprise, and as I have mentioned previously, I discovered that the Bible discusses economic issues more than prayer. Now, what does that mean for my life?

The themes of faith, work, and economics—the key to living as an eight-sided disciple—were explored in the first three pillars of the catechism. The last five pillars build upon the first three like foundation stones. Let's see what these might add to the experience of an eight-sided church: baptism, communion, confession (the Office of the Keys), blessings, and the Table of Duties.

7

Building Eighth-Day Disciples

Five More Foundational Keys for Mission and Ministry

> We have moved to a recession that will be worse than the
> one we experienced in 2008 . . . and our social fabric and
> cohesion is under stress.
> —Amina J. Mohammed, UN deputy-secretary general

> Given the nature of the crisis, all hands should be on
> deck, all available tools should be used.
> —Christine Lagarde, president of the
> European Central Bank

The first three pillars of the *Small Catechism* provide ample resources for living on the eighth day of creation. The Ten Commandments (law), the Apostles' Creed (the Triune God as good news), and the Lord's Prayer (God's kingdom and economy)—proclaimed in that order—are beautiful gifts for God's people. The *Small Catechism* goes further, however, in pointing Christians to five more architectural elements or tools for living as eighth-day disciples. These tools are baptism, communion, confession (the Office of the Keys), blessings, and the Table of Duties.

Do you and your congregation really need all eight catechetical resources for the building up of your spiritual life? The answer is yes. Let me explain. If you play golf, you could play eighteen holes with only five clubs. You could, for example, use the driver, the three wood for fairways, the five iron, the nine iron, and the putter. Any difficult golf course, however, is laid out to force a golfer to use all the clubs. That's the challenge! Certain holes are laid out specifically to force golfers to reach deep into their bags. In the end, to play well, you need more than five clubs.

The same is true for a good set of tools. A few tools are always needed, such as a hammer, screwdriver, wrench, saw, and measuring tape. But difficult jobs demand all the tools in the set! That's the beauty of having a complete set of tools. You are ready for any job.

Kitchens work the same way. Sure, you can cook a simple meal with just a few pots and pans, a set of knives, and some basic appliances. But what if you are called on to cook a specialized dish for a family of twenty at Christmas? A well-stocked kitchen has the necessary equipment to cook any dish for any occasion.

The same principle is true for the eight parts of the catechism. For Christian discipleship, we need all God's gifts. To explore these five additional gifts for living as disciples within the eighth day of creation, we begin with the two sacraments recognized by most Protestant churches, the sacraments of baptism and communion (sometimes referred to as the Sacrament of the Altar). The overarching question that remains at the forefront of our study is this: What do the sacraments teach us about how to connect faith, work, and economics on Monday within the eighth-day story of creation?

The same process used above will be employed in this section as well. First, Luther's teaching on each section in the *Small Catechism* will be outlined by the use of questions and answers. Afterward, a faith, work, and economics (FWE) commentary will be offered.[1]

THE SACRAMENT OF HOLY BAPTISM

1

What is baptism?
Baptism is not simply plain water. Instead, it is water used according to God's command and connected with God's word.

What then is this word of God?
Where our Lord Christ says in Matthew 28, "Go therefore and make disciples of all nations, baptizing them in the name of the Father and of the Son and of the Holy Spirit."

2

What gifts or benefits does baptism grant?
It brings about forgiveness of sins, redeems from death and the devil, and gives eternal salvation to all who believe it, as the words and promises of God declare.

What are these words and promises of God?
Where our Lord Christ says in Mark 16, "The one who believes and is baptized will be saved; but the one who does not believe will be condemned."

3

How can water do such great things?
Clearly the water does not do it, but the word of God, which is with and alongside the water, and faith, which trusts this word of God in the water. For without the word of God the water is plain water and not a baptism, but with word of God it is a baptism, that is, a grace-filled water of life and a "bath of the new birth in the Holy Spirit," as St. Paul says to Titus in chapter 3, "through the water of rebirth and renewal by the Holy Spirit. This Spirit he poured out on us richly through Jesus Christ our Savior, so that, having been justified by his grace, we might become heirs according to the hope of eternal life. The saying is sure" (Tit 3:5–8).

4

What then is the significance of such a baptism with water?
It signifies that the old person in us with all sins and evil desires is to be drowned and die through daily sorrow for sin and through repentance, and on the other hand that daily a new person is to come forth and rise up to live before God in righteousness and purity forever.

Where is this written?

St. Paul says in Romans 6, "We are buried with Christ by baptism into death, so that, just as Christ was raised from the dead by the glory of the Father, so we too might walk in newness of life."

FWE Commentary

In baptism, God bestows gifts. As we get wet, God gives gifts through words of promise spoken to us! Specifically, God is the gift, a relationship with Father, Son, and Holy Spirit. "To know Christ is to know his benefits," as Philip Melanchthon, Luther's friend and colleague, famously wrote.[2] Thus, in baptism, we are baptized into God's very life with all its benefits and all its responsibilities. This action represents an actual adoption as children of God, which comes with an inheritance. God's work becomes our work. God's mission becomes our mission. God's spirit is given to us freely. Luther speaks of "forgiveness of sins, life, and salvation." We may hear about this call to mission on Sunday, but the gifts we receive from God are meant to be enjoyed and employed on Monday. God is working through us to love the world starting on Monday morning. *Love* here also means to govern, to cocreate, to steward, to administer. Thus, being adopted by God makes us participants in the Triune God's grand home economics project. Theological language has various ways of talking about God's new economy in Christ. Terms like *God's mission, God's kingdom,* and *living in faith* or *in the Spirit* are common. The language used at the baptismal font—or at the riverbank—is that the baptized are now drawn into the big drama of God's work and rest on both Sunday and Monday. In baptism, we have been called, claimed, and cleansed. God's call to us through water and words of promise changes everything. A simplistic way to express this is as follows: God's gifts and call celebrated on Sunday are meant for Monday. This is a simplistic formulation because God gives gifts to us every day. Prayer sanctifies every day of the week and makes it holy. Each day then becomes the eighth day of creation. That's what baptism teaches us.

Therefore, although baptism happens but once, the experience of baptism—being renewed by the Holy Spirit through the forgiveness afforded us through death and resurrection—should be a daily experience. Practicing confession and receiving forgiveness is the basic act of being a Christian. Many Christians cross themselves daily or regularly to remember the experience of God's eternal life given to them as a gift every day. Each day, we are reminded that we are called, claimed, cleansed, and made anew. Why? To serve God's new economy in Christ through our daily work.

THE SACRAMENT OF COMMUNION
(OR THE SACRAMENT OF THE ALTAR)

What is the Sacrament of the Altar?
It is the true body and blood of our Lord Jesus Christ under the bread and wine, instituted by Christ himself for us Christians to eat and drink.

Where is this written?
The holy evangelists Matthew, Mark, and Luke, and St. Paul write thus: "In the night in which he was betrayed, our Lord Jesus took bread, and gave thanks, broke it, and gave it to his disciples, saying: Take and eat; this is my body, given for you. Do this for the remembrance of me. Again, after supper, he took the cup, gave thanks, and gave it for all to drink, saying: This cup is the new covenant in my blood, shed for you and for all people for the forgiveness of sin. Do this for the remembrance of me."

What is the benefit of such eating and drinking?
The words "given for you" and "shed for you for the forgiveness of sin" show us that forgiveness of sin, life, and salvation, are given to us in the sacrament through these words, because where there is forgiveness of sin, there is also life and salvation.

How can bodily eating and drinking do such a great thing?
Eating and drinking certainly do not do it, but rather the words that are recorded: "given for you" and "shed for you for the forgiveness

of sin." These words, when accompanied by the physical eating and drinking, are the essential thing in the sacrament, and whoever believes these very words has what they declare and state, namely, "forgiveness of sins."

Who, then, receives this sacrament worthily?
Fasting and bodily preparation are in fact a fine external discipline, but a person who has faith in these words, "given for you" and "shed for you for the forgiveness of sin," is really worthy and well prepared. However, a person who does not believe these words or doubts them is unworthy and unprepared, because the words "for you" require truly believing hearts.

FWE Commentary
Whereas baptism represents a onetime declaration of God's adoption like the Jewish practice of circumcision, communion is a repeated invitation to and experience of the kingdom. This invitation happens "as often as we come together" in remembrance of our Lord. When we gather around bread and wine, we remember Jesus. We remember Christ's life, death, and resurrection. We remember his act of sacrifice and his forgiveness. We remember his promise to be with us always. Above all, we recognize that Jesus hosts this meal.

Baptism represents God's call and claim on our lives. It's permanent. Communion, in contrast, is a regular invitation to fellowship around God's table. Each week—or daily—Jesus invites us to his table for "a foretaste of the feast to come." Like the Lord's Prayer, celebrating the Lord's Supper is a communal experience. We receive it worthily when we approach God as sinners. We are worthy when we believe that Jesus's words to us are true: "I died for you. You are forgiven." Amen!

The apex of the communion liturgy is the words of institution: "given and shed for you for the forgiveness of sin." Jesus offers us his whole self with these words and, as Luther articulates it, he does this gospel gifting with bread and wine, eating and drinking. Salvation is the gift: Jesus for you!

Concerning work and economics, the meaning of whole eucharistic liturgy begins with the offering. In response to the word of God read and preached, the congregation offers gifts of thanksgiving with symbols from Monday's activities: bread, wine, and money. Money represents the fruit of our labors. Bread represents the constructive work of our hands. Wine represents our creativity and joy. A tithe isn't sufficient here. The symbols brought to the altar represent our whole lives. We offer them to the Lord in gratitude, knowing that they are inadequate and tainted by sin. Jesus receives our offerings, makes them holy through his word, and gives them back as his body and blood, "for you." This "gift exchange" represents the whole rhythm of the sacrament. The exchange lies at the heart of God's economy. God gives us Godself. What God desires in exchange is that we "thank and praise, serve and obey him," as it states in the explanation of the Apostles' Creed. If we get this gift exchange wrong, it leads to works righteousness—that is, we are trying to pay for forgiveness or earn God's pleasure with our discipleship. In such cases, we haven't heard the gospel correctly. If we get it right, our lives reflect faith and obedience. All is a gift!

One point here is often overlooked. The gifts from the table are for the life of the world, and not just the church. If the church consumes everything from the table, then it has not understood the message of the kingdom and God's economy. Passivity too cannot be the fruit of this tree. Otherwise, those around the table have not understood the vision of God's new economy in Christ. The experience at the table inspires God's people to serve their neighbors in new ways. Communion models how God's economy works. In fact, the Eucharist actually "does" God's economy. The communion experience teaches us how faith in the kingdom relates to daily life. It first creates the community of the church—the *new creation*. Then it sends that new community out into the world to share its gifts for the life of the world.

CONFESSION

What is confession?

Confession consists of two parts. One is that we confess our sins. The other is that we receive "the absolution," that is, forgiveness, from the pastor as from God himself and by no means doubt but firmly believe that our sins are thereby forgiven before God in heaven.

Which sins is a person to confess?

Before God one is to acknowledge the guilt for all sins, even those of which we are not aware, as we do in the Lord's Prayer. However, before the pastor we are to confess only those sins of which we have knowledge, and which trouble us.

Which sins are these?

Here reflect on your place in life in light of the Ten Commandments: whether you are father, mother, son, daughter, master, mistress, servant; whether you have been disobedient, unfaithful, lazy; whether you have harmed anyone by word or deed; whether you have stolen, neglected, wasted, or injured anything.

FWE Commentary

Luther taught the practice of absolution and confession (otherwise known as the Office of the Keys) within the context of a person's various vocations. Confession and absolution act like keys; they open doors in each area of a person's life—family, work, church, and community. Christians are therefore to pray the Ten Commandments regularly to see where we, in our call to love God and serve our neighbor, have missed the mark. People can pray the Ten Commandments most effectively with specific references to their daily lives. The Ten Commandments, for example, are applied to my various calls at home and in the office, through civic engagement, or at church. If I'm a student, I'm thinking about life at school. Sins are confessed from these particular settings. Then that person receives the words of absolution from Scripture directly, or from a priest, a pastor, a member of the family, a friend, or anyone who is willing to proclaim with confidence Jesus's words of forgiveness.

The rite of confession and absolution can be practiced alone during private prayer, in a collective environment in worship, or one-on-one. To begin and end each day with forgiveness is important. Forgiveness changes the way we approach our various callings. Forgiveness can even help us sleep at night. In essence, the practice of absolution and confession is the practice of evangelism, a gospel word targeted to those specific areas of unbelief in our daily lives. The bottom line is that the practice of confession and absolution should be tied to our daily vocations.

We fully enter the eighth day of creation through confession and absolution, death and resurrection. That is why confession and absolution are understood as the keys to the kingdom.

MORNING AND EVENING BLESSINGS

How the head of the house is to teach the members of the household to say morning and evening blessings:

The Morning Blessing
In the morning, as soon as you get out of bed, you are to make the sign of the holy cross and say:
God the Father, Son, and Holy Spirit watch over me. Amen.
Then, kneeling or standing, say the Apostles' Creed and the Lord's Prayer. If you wish, you may in addition recite this little prayer as well:
I give thanks to you, heavenly Father, through Jesus Christ your dear Son, that you have protected me through the night from all harm and danger. I ask that you would also protect me today from sin and all evil, so that my life and actions may please you. Into your hands I commend myself: my body, my soul, and all that is mine. Let your holy angel be with me, so that the wicked foe may have no power over me.

After singing a hymn, or whatever else may serve your devotion, you are to go to your work joyfully.

The Evening Blessing
In the evening, when you go to bed, you are to make the sign of the holy cross and say:

God the Father, Son, and Holy Spirit watch over me. Amen.

Then, kneeling or standing, say the Apostles' Creed and the Lord's Prayer. If you wish, you may recite this little prayer as well:

I give thanks to you, heavenly Father, through Jesus Christ your dear Son, that you have graciously protected me today. I ask you to forgive me all my sins, where I have done wrong, and graciously to protect me tonight. Into your hands I commend myself: my body, my soul, and all that is mine. Let your holy angel be with me, so that the wicked foe may have no power over me. Amen.

Then you are to go to sleep quickly and cheerfully.

Blessings at Meals
How the head of the house is to teach members of the household to offer blessing and thanksgiving at meals.

The Table Blessings
The children and the members of the household are to come devoutly to the table, fold their hands, and recite:

The eyes of all wait upon you, O Lord, and you give them their food in due season. You open your hand and satisfy the desire of every living creature.

Then they are to recite the Lord's Prayer and the following prayer:

Lord God, heavenly Father, bless us and these your gifts, which we receive from your bountiful goodness, through Jesus Christ our Lord. Amen.

Thanksgiving

Similarly, after eating they should in the same manner fold their hands and recite devoutly:

Give thanks to the Lord, for the Lord is good, for God's mercy endures forever. God provides food for the cattle and for the young ravens when they cry. God is not impressed by the might of a horse and has no pleasure in the speed of a runner, but finds pleasure in those who fear the Lord, in those who await God's steadfast love.

Then recite the Lord's Prayer and the following prayer:

We give thanks to you, Lord God our Father, through Jesus Christ our Lord for all your benefits, you who live and reign forever. Amen.

FWE Commentary

Every day is sanctified by prayer. Our work is sanctified by prayer. Our schoolwork and church work are sanctified by prayer. Our family life is sanctified by prayer. So we begin and end each day with prayer: "Lord bless this day." The same is true for our meals. What better way to acknowledge God than by saying a blessing over every meal and ending each meal with a word of thanksgiving.

Luther learned how "to bless" and "to give thanks" in the monastery. He practiced both with the monks in accordance with biblical teaching. In the catechism, he passes along this ancient spiritual practice for our daily use.

An example: At the beginning of each day, we pray the Lord's Prayer. In this prayer, we ask for daily bread. At every meal then we acknowledge that our daily bread is now in front of us as a gift from God. Our petition is, "Lord, bless these gifts. Make them holy through prayer." After the meal, we return thanks to God for the gifts that we've enjoyed. These prayers ground us in gratitude, and not just for our food. Our gratitude now extends to every dimension of our family, work, and economy. All work by a Christian disciple begins with "blessing" and ends with "thanksgiving."

The spiritual practices around the kitchen table should also be practiced at work and at home. We ask God to bless our work. Afterward, we give thanks for the blessings we have received through our home, family, car, health care, doctors and nurses, food, shelter, work, paychecks, benefits, good government, roads, schools, great friends, police, military protection, local stores that provide every want, entertainment, healthy business environments, and more. We bless God's gifts. We thank God for rich provision.

THE TABLE OF DUTIES (OR THE HOUSEHOLD CHART OF SOME BIBLICAL PASSAGES)

Through these verses, all kinds of holy orders and walks of life may be admonished, as through lessons particularly pertinent to their office and duty.[3]

For Bishops, Pastors, and Preachers
Now a bishop must be above reproach, married only once, temperate, sensible, respectable, hospitable, an apt teacher, not a drunkard, not violent but gentle, not quarrelsome, and not a lover of money. (1 Tim 3:2–3)

Concerning Governing Authorities
Let every person be subject to the governing authorities; for there is no authority except from God, and those authorities that exist have been instituted by God. Therefore whoever resists authority resists what God has appointed, and those who resist will incur judgment. . . . It is the servant of God to execute wrath on the wrongdoer. (Rom 13:1–2, 4b)

For Husbands
Husbands, in the same way, show consideration for your wives in your life together, . . . so that nothing may hinder your prayers. (1 Pet 3:7)

Husbands, love your wives and never treat them harshly. (Col 3:19)

For Wives
Wives, in the same way, accept the authority of your husbands. (1 Pet 3:1)

For Parents
And, fathers, do not provoke your children to anger, but bring them up in the discipline and instruction of the Lord. (Eph 6:4)

For Children
Children, obey your parents in the Lord, for this is right. "Honor your father and mother"—this is the first commandment with a promise: "so that it may be well with you, and you may live long on the earth." (Eph 6:1–3)

For Employees
You employees, be obedient to your bosses with respect and cooperation, with singleness of heart, as to Christ himself; not with service meant only for the eyes, done as people-pleasers, but rather as servants of Christ, so that you do the will of God from the heart [with good attitude]. Imagine to yourselves that you are serving the Lord and not people, and know that whatever good anyone does, the same will that person receive, whether servant or free. (based on Eph 6:5–8)

For Employers
And, bosses, do the same to them. Stop threatening them, for you know that both of you have the same Master in heaven, and with him there is no partiality. (based on Eph 6:9)

For Young People in General
In the same way, you who are younger must accept the authority of the elders. And all of you must clothe yourselves with

humility in your dealings with one another, for "God opposes the proud, but gives grace to the humble." Humble yourselves therefore under the mighty hand of God, so that he may exalt you in due time. (1 Pet 5:5–6)

For Widows
The real widow, left alone, has set her hope on God and continues in supplications and prayers night and day; but the widow who lives for pleasure is dead even while she lives. (1 Tim 5:5–6)

For All in the Community
The commandments . . . are summed up in this word, "Love your neighbor as yourself." (Rom 13:9)

First of all, then, I urge that supplications, prayers, intercessions, and thanksgivings be made for everyone. (1 Tim 2:1)

Let all their lessons be learned with care,
So that the household well may fare.

FWE Commentary
How do I live within the eighth day of creation by faith? The Table of Duties provides Christians with scriptural admonitions for how to live their lives as followers of Jesus on Monday. This part of the catechism is divided into sections that correspond with various calls or vocations. Each vocation is peppered with scriptural passages so that we can learn and be inspired by how Christians in the past made connections between their faith and their daily lives.

Warning: Today's word of grace can quickly become an unhelpful "law" tomorrow. Manna is only good for one day, as the children of Israel learned in the wilderness. This can happen with scriptural admonitions as well. A word of instruction to Christians in the first century might not apply in the same way today. These examples from Scripture, however, inform us of how Christians in the past lived out their lives of discipleship and how we might learn from their examples. Every congregation should work hard to show how Scripture can be used to connect the word of God to their daily vocations. Which words from Scripture speak to our vocational challenges today? This is not easy work for a pastor, a teacher, or any Christian disciple. Learning to use Scripture evangelically is fundamental for living faithfully as an eighth-day disciple. Abandoning Scripture as "irrelevant for the modern world" will prove harmful in the end. On the flip side, not every text applies directly to today. Some were meant for Moses or Paul or the congregation at Ephesus, not us. Ultimately, the purpose of the Scriptures is to drive us to a life of faith and service. The word of God is about creating faith and life in the Spirit. The Bible is not meant to be used primarily as an ethical rulebook or a how-to manual. It's a book of faith.

Consequently, living on the eighth day means living by faith. This is the life that pleases God. Faith thrives in freedom, not with to-do lists of laws to complete. Whether we are acting out of the "musts" of commandments or out of the freedom of faith is always a matter of discernment. It is this discernment that represents how we build an architecture of discipleship. Our goal is to connect faith in God's promises with work and economics. Faith works in freedom to serve both God and neighbor.

Finally, the Table of Duties is focused on the various vocational roles we play in our families, communities, and churches. Additional passages may be added—and some subtracted—to any list used within a congregation to teach Christians about how to live out their callings in response to God's economy.

USING ALL YOUR EVANGELICAL TOOLS

The architectural elements of baptism, communion, confession (the Office of the Keys), blessings, and the Table of Duties are all fundamental to living the life of discipleship. An eight-sided spirituality needs all the basics to be strong, resilient, and grounded in the gospel. When we eliminate any one of these eight elements, we lose an important architectural piece of the structure of the building. When we face storms, we need a solid home. Discipleship, in the end, needs all eight architectural features of the catechism to thrive and prosper.

Just like the clubs in a golf bag, the tools in a toolbox, or the utensils in a well-equipped kitchen, God has given us amazing gifts so that we can live the life of faith. To live within an eight-sided church, we need to be taught about each and every one of these gifts. We thank God that we've been given all the tools necessary to live within the eighth day, to participate in the new creation.

8

Eighth-Day Discipleship in an Eight-Sided Church

Living by Faith with Responsibility and Freedom

> Most of our social and economic ideals come from Christianity or are derived from it. . . . It is surprising how much the economy has in common with the Old and New Testaments. . . . In fact, the key concepts of Christianity would not make sense without economic terminology. . . . And so, it appears that the basic messages of Christianity can be better understood in our economic age if they are interpreted in the (original) economic terminology.
> —Tomáš Sedláček, *The Economics of Good and Evil*

One of my biggest fears in life is that, when faced with a genuine crisis, I won't act quickly enough. Leadership as an unanxious presence is my default position. Calm leadership is usually appropriate. At other times, however, immediate and bold action saves lives. Slow decisions prove costly. Military officers confirm this tension between calm and bold action in war. Doctors share similar stories about patients. Leaders must make timely decisions. Lives depend on it.

Faced with significant headwinds today, and in response to Jesus's call to discipleship, congregational leaders must act! Laissez-faire leadership leaves weak communities. The call today, the apostolic call, is to eighth-day discipleship. Lives are at stake.

Acting quickly and appropriately in a crisis means more than just "rocking the boat." Our mandate as church leaders isn't just to scream out prophetic monologues from the pulpit or to cry "fire" in a crowded, or not so crowded, church building. Once the storms are recognized, how does a responsible leader—a good shepherd—guide the flock to new and greener pastures?

My first response to this leadership challenge is to become a better storyteller. Storytelling doesn't equal passivity. Just the opposite. The call to "better storytelling" is a recognition that Christian communities need more poetry and fewer church-growth techniques. A story is a powerful tool. It draws you in. Within its narrative framework, you discover your own identity, community, and purpose.[1] Once you find yourself in the story, the story itself acts like the preacher, the teacher, and the community organizer. The story can likewise teach you to become an architect, forming you as you live life under its canopy. This is the power of the eighth day of creation story. This story is a drama that you are invited to enter by faith. It's good news! Identity, community, and purpose are all found under its roof.

HOW DO I TELL THE EIGHT-SIDED STORY WELL?

Any approach to "making disciples" today must revolve around a gospel story that links a person's faith with their work and economic lives. Making these connections is essential. Attempts at Christian formation within our families, schools, places of work, and congregations that avoid these basic themes will leave people vulnerable. We don't want people building their lives on sandy soil. The storms are coming! The viruses are already in our communities. Sunday must never end up being divorced from Monday, or our work will quickly become flat and grind on without spiritual purpose. Is this not already the experience of many people we know? Why? Laissez-faire spiritual formation has proven to be limited in scope and deficient in substance. I speak from my own past deficiencies as a congregational leader. Houston, we have a problem! So let the prophets motivate us all again.

Christians who have already experienced the divorce between Sunday and Monday will find it hard to grasp God's grand narrative in Christ. They will struggle to comprehend how important their work is within the salvation story. Faith is the lens through which a person can see this amazing cosmic drama unfolding. Faith sees—even through a glass darkly—what's happening on God's grand stage. Faith gives us ears to hear God's invitation to act in the drama. Faith reveals that, in Christ, your work matters to God's economy.

Our neighbors have also been called to play a role within God's grand home economics project. They have been redeemed. Their debts have been forgiven. God invites them to respond to the call. Vocation is a marvelous gateway into evangelism. The key to grasping the catechetical vision of how the word of God works is that Luther is first telling a story as good news. Second, he is telling a story over against other competing stories. The gospel story always openly clashes with other worldviews. So the evangelical story must be told with precision so that the contrasts to other worldviews can be clearly understood. I mentioned some of these counternarratives in earlier chapters:

- moralistic therapeutic deism
- *homo economicus*
- the prosperity gospel
- radical tribalism

Furthermore, these counternarratives have a strong economic component. How could it be otherwise in our culture, which so deeply values economic issues? What these alternative worldviews promise economically at first sounds whimsical. Like good news. This means that if the economic side of the biblical story isn't told clearly and authoritatively, these counternarratives win, replacing the eighth-day gospel in people's lives.

Luther's evangelical story is a story about the eighth day. It's the story of Christ sitting on the throne at the right hand of the Father, managing God's economy. This is the kingdom of God. Luther's *Small Catechism* is an eighth-day discipleship manual that teaches how a Christian is to move by faith through the week, motivated and inspired by the grand narrative of the Triune God's kingdom work. As such, this catechism defines evangelical faith in ways that connect our work and our economic lives to the Lordship of Jesus Christ.

PAINTING GOD'S ECONOMIC STORY

How can a good storyteller make the gospel story's connections with the intricate dynamics of "faith, work, and economics" more understandable? One answer is to use art. So let's initiate an art class that is theologically informed.

Take out paints and brushes. Select a canvas. Sit quietly. Reflect deeply. Your challenge is to paint a picture of God. Don't be intimidated by the exercise. The theme is big. Just approach the activity like a child: spontaneously. How do you see or understand God? Take your time. First, get a picture in your head. Imagine God's activities in the world. What images come to mind?

I tried this exercise myself. The first image that came to mind was an old man with a beard. I knew better, of course. God's not a man. God doesn't have a beard either. I just didn't know how else to start. I sketched out a cross at the center of the painting. Jesus in robes. A dove was added, but as an afterthought. As I stood back and reflected on my composition, I realized that my "grand narrative" didn't have the world as its landscape. My own neighborhood wasn't depicted. Even my family was absent. Furthermore, there were no magi from the East. No shepherds in the fields keeping watch over their flocks by night. No Roman Empire as a threat to the community. My grand narrative of redemption was small and limited.

Upon reflection, I have concluded that before 2012, my painting would have definitely reduced the grand redemptive narrative even further, to a picture of people of faith largely escaping this world—this veil of tears—and reuniting with Christ in heaven. My painting would have shown the world much like the *Titanic*, with me, the pastor, throwing life preservers heroically over the rails to my people struggling in the cold water below.

My painting before 2012 did not extend its lines, images, or colors to a story of God's reign over all the world but rather just to a few individual people struggling to escape the world. Furthermore, my story of salvation would not have included "regular jobs" from Monday through Saturday. Although I knew better intellectually, I would not have included work scenes in my painting, or neighborhoods within my city, or other religions and regions of the world, for that matter. The picture of the gospel story I preached and taught would not have filled a large expansive canvas. Did I have an eighth-day vision of the story of redemption? Definitely not! The new creation played no role. Heaven was the ultimate goal. Salvation meant escape and eternal rest, not engagement with the world.

So how is your painting taking shape? Does your canvas reflect God's economic activities in the world? Is your own work included? Furthermore, if your congregation were to paint that picture together, as a group project, what would be the result?

PAINTING YOUR PICTURE AS A GROUP

Let's get more specific. It's really your group picture of God that lies behind every activity of your congregation, from how you do worship on Sunday to how you work in the neighborhood, from how you allocate budgetary funds to how you organize the fellowship time. Consequently, you need to pay attention to the details of your group picture.

- What does God look like?
- Is God passive or active?
- Where is God on the page?
- Does God seem happy or angry?
- Is God on a throne or suffering?
- What role does God play? Is God, for example, a king, a servant, a doctor, a host at a party, an activist, a child, a judge, a shepherd, a teacher, a homeless person, a physician, a beggar?
- How is Jesus painted? Did the Holy Spirit get painted?
- Is God involved with the local economy? With local businesses? With families?

- Finally, what is God doing—acts of justice, healing, comfort, feeding the poor, peace? And what work, if any, are you doing?

The truth is, although it may sound somewhat fanciful, this art project is absolutely critical to forming disciples of Jesus. We act on our images of God. Narratives are even more powerful than theological statements. This is true no matter where those pictures originate or how "truthful" they are. Our pictures of God guide our lives, for good or ill. This is true for every person, Christian or not. It is also true for groups, families, and businesses too. Even nations. Our focus here is on congregations. Check your mission statement as a church. This statement has a picture of God in it. It tells a story. So too does your church budget. Can you see it? Can you hear it? Remember, numbers always tell a story. What role does the biblical story play in your picture? Is there something in the picture that reflects "good news" for the world, something worth telling others about?

"Economics" can assist in shaping our art project because economics describes God's big plan for creating, redeeming, and stewarding the world. Economics, therefore, drives us back to the grand narrative of the Bible. Now look at your painting again. How is God's economic grand narrative reflected in your painting of God? With this picture, can you be a good storyteller?

Finally, does your group painting reflect more the biblical story or one of the compelling counternarratives? Be truthful.

GOD'S ECONOMIC STORY BETWEEN EDEN AND THE NEW JERUSALEM

Good teaching should assist us in forming our picture of God. Preaching helps us "see" and "paint." How does the preacher in your congregation use the Bible to paint the picture of God? Do the preachers and teachers use a catechism? The study of God's economics is influenced fundamentally by two biblical stories—the bookend stories of Eden and the New Jerusalem. The Bible begins with the first story about a garden and ends with a final story about a city. Economics is how God governs, stewards, and operates the world from the vantage point of these two ongoing places/events of creation (Eden) and new creation (the New Jerusalem). And as we discovered in the Genesis story, creation stories, both new and old, always come with vocational calls to achieve a mission. God creates. God calls us to work in God's mission.

These two Bible stories are meant to frame our understanding of reality. "Eden" and "the New Jerusalem" are thus determinate stories about God's interaction with us and the world. When we talk about "the economy," we are really telling a story or painting a picture. Eden and New Jerusalem are biblical stories that will consequently emerge in every story we tell and every picture we paint. That's why the Bible places these stories in such prominent positions at the beginning and at the end.

GETTING "REST" AND "WORK" RIGHT IN THE GRAND STORY OF REDEMPTION

Another central theme within God's big redemption story is the relationship between work and rest. One whole commandment is dedicated to this theme. The Apostles' Creed also has the work-and-rest relationship at its heart. Has there ever been a time when Sabbath rest is more needed than today? Or resurrection work? It is hard not to read any book about Sabbath rest without feeling inspired to change one's lifestyle. One should never forget, however, that Sabbath rest and Monday work must always stand side-by-side. God's call to work exists alongside God's call to rest. One can't exist without the other.

Practicing Sabbath usually starts by reserving one day in which you do no work. Some go even further, calling for dopamine fasts. *Sabbath rest spirituality* is defined broadly today and extends from taking regular vacations to taking a "rest" from technology, from dedicating daily quiet time for prayer and meditation to finding generative moments for celebration and joy. In our hectic daily lives, any word about how to rest comes as good news. Discovering that God actually commands us to rest is almost shocking in its power and impact: "Thou shalt rest!"

The rest and work dimensions of the redemption story should always be viewed together. The interactive relationship between these twin motifs makes all the difference in how the grand story of redemption is told, heard, and experienced. Experiencing the benefits of salvation depends on getting this relationship right. Confusion about the proper relationship between rest and work is one of the reasons the sixteenth-century Reformation was so important. Rest and work, consequently, can be understood in ways that are evangelical or nonevangelical. Small distinctions, when overlooked, can lead to huge problems.

It's so easy to get distracted as we strive to be relevant. The *Small Catechism* pushes back against this temptation to diminish or abandon the gospel story of rest-and-work on the altar of "cultural relevance." This catechism walks us through a holistic eight-sided presentation of the story of redemption chapter by chapter.

THE GOSPEL AND ECONOMIC THRIVING: THREE STORIES

Faith and economics are realities that always function together. Once a person starts to see the connection, it changes their whole way of hearing Jesus's call to discipleship. Three examples of this linkage will be described below. These illustrations have been chosen because they point to the range of possibilities for every Christian community that should be explored. They have also greatly influenced me. One example is from the Reformation, one from the liturgical tradition of Christian worship, and one from Philadelphia, the city of brotherly love.

Luther and the Community Chest

We start with history. The Reformation sparked economic prosperity in various German cities. Others throughout Europe then replicated the innovations of Wittenberg so that they might similarly thrive.

Are we surprised by this connection between faith and economics? Admittedly, yes. Did my Lutheran church teach me the vital link between faith and economics as I studied my Reformation heritage? The simple answer is no—or was I not prepared to hear the connection at the time? This financial side of the Reformation needs to be retold today. The time is right.

Carter Lindberg describes this dimension of Luther's life. Let me quote heavily from Lindberg's article because he has done a marvelous job of mixing together important historical references with Luther quotes:

> Faith active in love rooted in God's promise and testament is experienced in worship. The "sacrament is rightly called a fountain of love." Playing on the word of worship, "Gottesdienst" [worship service or service to God], Luther states, "Now there is no greater service of God [Dienst Gottis] than Christian love which helps and serves the needy, as Christ himself will judge and testify at the Last Day, Matthew 25 [31–46]." For Luther social ethics flows from worship; it is the "liturgy after the liturgy"; that is how a Christian acts. He is conscious of nothing else than that the goods which are his are also given to his neighbor. He makes no distinction but helps everyone with body and life, goods and honor, as much as he can. Faith active in love is indeed personal, but not privatistic. Worship and social welfare are inseparable.
>
> Under the rubric of Deuteronomy 15:4, "there will be no poor among you," Luther and his Wittenberg colleagues proceeded to establish social welfare programs. Luther was concerned to develop prophylactic as well as remedial social assistance, "For so to help a man that he does not need to become a beggar is just as much of a good work and a virtue as to give alms to a man who has already become a beggar" (LW 13:54).
>
> The first social welfare ordinance, the "Common Purse" (Beutelordnung), was passed by the Wittenberg Town Council with Luther's assistance in late 1520 or early 1521. "The

charitable gifts were to be collected in church and distributed to the local poor. Where possible, a surplus of grain and wood should be collected for distribution in times of need. The new arrangement of charity appears to have begun to function in Wittenberg immediately." The next major step influenced by Luther was the Wittenberg Order of January 1522. It is known as the "Common Chest" because a chest for the weekly collection and disbursement of funds was built with three separate locks and keys. Four stewards were elected on the basis of their knowledge of the town and the citizens' needs. The only criterion for distribution of loans or outright gifts was to be the need of the recipient. Initially, funded by expropriated ecclesiastical endowments and then by taxes, gifts, and wills, the Wittenberg Order prohibited begging (directed at the Mendicant Orders and swindlers); provided interest-free loans to artisans, who when established were to repay them if possible; provided for poor orphans, the children of poor people, and poor woman in need of dowries for marriage; provided refinancing of high-interest loans at 4 percent annual interest for burdened citizens; supported the education of vocational training for poor children; and vocational retraining for under-employed artisans. The Common Chest also soon added the services of the physician Melchior Fendt (1486–1564). Paid by the Common Chest, he worked as town physician on behalf of the poor. In addition to the expenses of the doctor and medications, the Common Chest paid for hot baths and bath cures for healing particular illnesses, along with hospitals for those with mental as well as physical maladies, and as such laid the foundation for the modern social health care system. The Common Chest functioned as a kind of central bank for communal poor relief that was now a responsibility of the state. It was a new institutional creation that had not existed anywhere prior to the Reformation. Well-provided and staffed, the Common Chest order introduced a "professionalization of social welfare" that became widespread and continued into the early nineteenth century. . . .

"The Wittenberg Common Chest quickly attracted the attention and emulation of cities with preachers influenced by Luther, including Augsburg, Nuremberg, and Altenburg in 1522, and Kitzingen, Strasbourg, Breslau, and Regensburg in 1523, as well as areas such as Hesse."[2]

Luther's discovery of the gospel ignited a whole new approach to economics in Wittenberg. Work was dignified and had a divine purpose. The church invested money and vocational training into their people. Worker-priests were formed and trained! Universities and libraries were founded along with vocational and public schools. The result was that the economy flourished. Work was understood as daily ministry to serve the neighbor in God's economy. The economy was one important place where "service" to the neighbor was practiced. Service to and love of neighbor therefore trumped individual self-interest. *Homo economicus* and greed were thus checked and constrained in Wittenberg. A new approach to the local economy was born as worship and service.

Evangelical Worship as an Economic Story

Worship is the place where faith and economics must be weekly taught and practiced. Sunday morning is the time and place where we celebrate "worship as service" and "service as worship." But how?

Liturgy establishes the architecture for worship. Liturgies are amazingly effective teachers. The movement of the classic liturgies is fascinating for what it teaches us, especially about how to connect faith, work, and economics today. Liturgy, at its core, tries to tell a story. Many people in the pews have never heard or understood the narrative flow of traditional liturgies. Traditional liturgical worship is often experienced unfortunately like a cafeteria line. There's no unified menu, just separate dishes. The negative consequences of overlooking the overarching story of the liturgy are evident in almost all churches that use traditional forms of worship. Without understanding the grand story that the liturgy is trying to tell, the worship experience is flattened and incomprehensible. It bores.

In Lutheran churches, the liturgical flow of worship follows the narrative flow of the catechism. It's an order of salvation. The worship experience starts by focusing on the word of God and ends with the experience of gathering at God's table. Word and sacrament form a unity. This movement is represented on most Sundays with two separate liturgies that form one powerful narrative of redemption:

The connections among faith, work, and economics play a role in the sermon, of course. The communion liturgy, however, is where the architectural connections can become even more visible and real. This becomes particularly clear right where the service of the word transitions and the communion liturgy begins—that is, in the offering.

Liturgy of the Word   Liturgy of Holy Communion

The role that the offering plays in the old traditional liturgies is surprisingly rich. Its function is not about collecting money. Rather, the offering functions as a bridge between the two liturgies of word and sacrament. Notice the language. It's not a "collection," it's an "offering." What is being offered to God is our service, prayers, and praise. Generosity flows from a heart freed up by the gospel. There's no pressure here. No philanthropic trickery. No guilt. After the gospel of Christ has been preached, people are ready to give. Generosity flows from a heart filled, one that has experienced good news.

The offering is an altar call, a call to discipleship, a call to die and live with Jesus. Jesus sits on the throne at the right hand of God, stewarding the whole world. Now Jesus invites us to join that stewardship work of the new creation. Like Adam and Noah, we are called to "till and work" the garden. We become worker-priests on Monday if we respond to this altar call on Sunday through the offering.

In the offering, we are called once again to hear Jesus's invitation, "Follow me." This means more than a mere tithe; 10 percent discipleship isn't sufficient. The cross of Christ represents more. God calls us to jump fully into the offering plate. Don't be surprised by this image.

As a sign of this full response to God's call, the symbols of bread, wine, and money are used to represent every dimension of our lives, our work, and our economies. All these gifts are brought forward as the fruit of our labor, our creativity and production, as well as our acts of joy and celebration. All these signs of our economies are placed on the altar for Jesus to sanctify. The first act of the new creation is that Jesus creates a new economy through his body and blood and creates among those gathered a new community. The experience enacted and received is one of death and new life.

With this small ritual "offering," an economic conversion takes place. Our work is transformed from a simple "job" into a calling from God to participate in the kingdom. Self-interest no longer dominates our efforts. Through Christ's call, our work and its fruits now become focused on service. The gift is the call. Daily work becomes a vocation in God's economy, an offering to God, an act of worship.

Fellowship around the communion table transforms the community's work into a call to serve on Mondays as worker-priests. This fellowship includes our offerings, which represent our gifts, our skills, and our productivity. God receives our sin-stained economic production and transforms it into God's very "real presence" in the world. The word of God performs this miracle. This is why the fellowship around the communion table—this exchange of gifts—is often called the Eucharist, the giving of thanks. The fellowship around the table is the invitation again to life on the eighth day of creation. As we receive Christ's body and blood around the table, faith transforms our daily work into a spiritual vocation of service within God's grand redemptive story for the world. Service to the neighbor becomes an act of grateful response to God's mercy in Christ. After all, God doesn't need our offering of money; our neighbor does. Around that altar, our daily work is transformed into kingdom service. As Gerhard Forde states, "Only when [the believer] is cured of his supernatural ambitions does he begin to see the natural. He receives creation back as a gift, and he can rejoice in it."[3]

The liturgy reflects the evangelical movement of the catechism. Liturgy is a story lived out as ritual. Each person plays a part in this eighth-day drama. The *Small Catechism* equipped those early

Reformers in Wittenberg to accept their daily work as worship, not Mass. The liturgy on Sunday uses the same form and substance to organize an evangelical experience. Good liturgy prepares people for their daily lives. Sunday and Monday are thus united at the altar.

John Wanamaker: Faith and the Retail World of Philadelphia

This twentieth-century story is about a giant personality who changed the retail world because he made the all-important connection between faith and economics. The story is about John Wanamaker. I lived in Philadelphia for several years right next to the store Wanamaker built as an architectural monument to his beliefs. His store reflected his spirituality, much like the eight-sided basilica in Philippi.

Wanamaker's store is now a Macy's on the corner of Thirteenth and Market Streets, right across from city hall. This magnificent store is described as a "cathedral to capitalism."[4] Preachers scoffed at its religious pretentiousness at the time. The building's architectural design looks and acts almost like all the octagonal churches across the world, with one exception. Wanamaker's cathedral is a retail store. It is true, his store was often filled with religious artwork and music, and employed the largest pipe organ in America.

Wanamaker tried to integrate his faith, his work, and his economic life in ways that can be easily observed. This attempt at "integration" contains good parts and bad. His weaknesses in hindsight are today easy to see. Wanamaker, however, changed the landscape of retail in America. Most of the realities associated with retail stores today have some connection to his innovations. Wanamaker's initiatives, most importantly, stemmed from his evangelical faith. Price tags, mood music, public art, social engagement with the city, store entertainment, training programs for workers, moral education through aesthetic design, and more all harkened back to how Wanamaker wanted his faith to influence the whole retail experience. A person's retail experience, for Wanamaker, had the potential to elevate their moral and spiritual life.

Wanamaker's story is important because we still live in the house that he built vis-à-vis retail shopping. This is true despite the recent shifts toward using online stores like Amazon. With Wanamaker, we can understand his store as an architectural model of his philosophy of life, which tried to integrate religious faith, business, art, architecture, and commerce in the United States.

Life was an integrated whole for Wanamaker. Sunday wasn't divorced from Monday. Wanamaker accepted the challenge to connect faith and economics in the public square to reform the urban landscape. He brought his religious commitments to his business commitments. He also brought his business acumen and finances to his religious engagement. The department store was his pulpit. Wanamaker emphasized "practical religion" as he proclaimed a "businessman's gospel."[5] He was trying to remake business in America into a Christian endeavor. A thriving life in the city of brotherly love would be the result.

Wanamaker's life was a sincere effort to integrate his faith, his work, and the economic life of Philadelphia. Did he succumb to the prosperity gospel? Yes, but one should be careful in comparing too closely what he preached through retail with our TV preachers today. Did he suffer from racism? Yes, he didn't escape the sins of his era. His strengths and weaknesses make Wanamaker's a compelling case study in how to connect, and not to connect, faith, work, and economics. His life represents a rich attempt at what an "integrated" life might mean within the business world and the public square.

On the December day that John Wanamaker died in 1922, the *Philadelphia Inquirer* published the following announcement on their front page: "World's Greatest Merchant and Philadelphia's Leader in Business, Philanthropy, Religion and Civic Effort Ends Brave Fight for Life."[6] Nicole C. Kirk describes the influence of his life in this way:

Wanamaker had changed the way people shopped, dined, and spent their free time. He had entered people's homes through the goods he sold—the fashions they wore, the furniture they selected, the art they hung on their walls—and the newspaper editorial advertisements he wrote six days a week. He had made fashion, music, art, history, and refinement accessible. He crafted public celebrations that were Christian and patriotic. He tried to make his story a "temple of culture." He provided educational opportunities and a path to bodily improvement that offered upward mobility for some of the thousands of young men and women who worked for him, while at the same time reinforcing racial and gender hierarchies that stymied the potential of African Americans, women, and immigrants. . . . He offered a vision of what people should be or, at the very least, what they could aspire to be. By doing so, he had become a tastemaker—a responsibility he felt was charged with religious and moral obligation that he took on with evangelistic zeal. It was an endeavor that also made him lots of money, which he understood as God's blessing. In many ways, he had achieved what he had set out to do—to morally uplift the city and commerce or, more specifically, at least some of its inhabitants.[7]

Wanamaker's story reflects a man of his era and culture. Inspiring. Flawed. Nevertheless, he is particularly striking as a person who tried to connect faith and economics at a time when most Protestants understood business as antithetical to religion. That is his powerful witness to us today. In the eyes of most Protestant leaders, business—especially retail business—remained spiritually problematic primarily due to its reputation for questionable ethics. When Wanamaker's friend, Dwight Moody, heard about his friend's move from ministry to business, he viewed the decision with disapproval. Moody wasn't the only dissenting voice. Business would only corrupt, they protested, and maybe even destroy Wanamaker's faith. We are all blessed that Wanamaker didn't accept Moody's advice. What if we all considered our place of employment our pulpit?

So what is your story? Where is your pulpit? How do you connect faith, work, and economics in your daily life? As you contemplate these critical questions, you might turn to catechism to help you stay grounded in the gospel story of the eighth day of creation and reject those false stories competing for your attention and loyalty. Might this be one lesson we can learn from Wanamaker? He needed a catechism in building his cathedral.

EVANGELICAL PRACTICES TODAY BASED ON THE *SMALL CATECHISM*

Being grounded in the eight "chapters" of the catechism can help defend us from the destructive stories that try to influence us every day. These eight tools or design elements can also lead to spiritual practices in our daily lives that touch our work and our economic relationships. They are practices that encourage us to live as eighth-day disciples. These are the eighth-day practices that have become important to me.

1. Become a Good Storyteller

Every pastor and congregation should commit to teaching their members as worker-priests how to tell the story of God's redemption in a compelling way. Good storytelling demands a new vocabulary and imagination. Emphasize the stories that help people connect faith, work (vocation), and economics. Christians need to be invited and encouraged to participate in God's home economics project. This big story of redemption should define our identity, our work, and our mission. Being a good storyteller means using creativity to tell the old, old scriptural story and to make explicit connections between it and the stories of our lives.

2. Practice Being a "Daily Baptist"

Baptism in water happens once. But the catechism encourages us to experience "death and resurrection," repentance and forgiveness, the "drowning of the old Adam [and Eve]" through the *daily* spiritual practice of confession and absolution. To practice daily baptism is to remember that we are called, claimed, and cleansed by God. Daily prayers might include absolution and confession twice a day, in the morning and in the evening. Thus, every day begins and ends with forgiveness. Learning to confess our sins is, in essence, learning how to become a Christian. Practicing daily baptism as repentance and forgiveness is an important expression of discipleship. Be a "daily baptist."

3. Practice Sabbath Rest and Work

A healthy spiritual life depends on how we connect faith and work. By consciously honoring the Sabbath, Christians practice holding a proper and godly relationship between work and rest. Practicing the Sabbath includes the following:

- Rest: Take a regular break from the tyranny of work, calendars, cell phones, the media, and all regular activities.
- Celebration: Celebrate God and God's gifts to you. Take time to enjoy the fruits of your labor and the accomplishments of the week.
- Renewal: Do those activities that renew and energize your life. This includes hearing the word of God in community above all. Experience spiritual rest. Read the Bible daily and practice confession and forgiveness.
- Blessing: Bless your family with shalom. Commit to reconciling relationships within your family, church fellowship, and friend groups. Stay connected to those you love.
- Hospitality: Bless your community with shalom by exercising hospitality to the neighbor and the stranger. Commit to reconciling relationships within your church community and neighborhood. Commit to the community.
- Work: Do "eighth-day" resurrection work—heal, liberate, free, empower, forgive, and do acts of mercy (Luke 13). Visit the sick, the homeless, the stranger. Invite people to dinner. Practice hospitality. Imagine a new local economy.

4. Pray the Catechism

The catechism is Christian teaching to be prayed daily. Pray the Ten Commandments, the Apostles' Creed, and the Lord's Prayer within the context of your family, work, civic duty, and church. The catechism is filled with tools for your daily vocational life within all the communities where you serve. Say blessings over your meals. Review God's guidance for your vocation in Scripture. Exercise daily confession and absolution. The catechism contains tools for spiritual warfare. Praying the catechism will change your attitude about your work and economic life.

5. Learn to Wield the Lord's Prayer

It's often been said that the Lord's Prayer is one of "the great martyrs of the earth." Whereas this may be true within formal worship services, and on football fields, it is also true that the Lord's Prayer is rarely used as a weapon for spiritual warfare during the week, at home, at school, or where we work. In its place, we try to find other more "relevant" economic prayers, such as the Prayer of Jabez. Tools become rusty when we don't learn to use them. A vibrant life of prayer needs the Lord's Prayer to guide it. When Jesus taught his disciples to pray, he taught them this prayer. Consequently, the Lord's Prayer should play a major role in our daily prayers. Many petitions to God can be misused without the Lord's Prayer to ground them.

6. Commit to Work as Your "Worship Service"

Living by faith frees a Christian for a life of service as worship. Protestant worship is understood as service. And service is understood as worship.[8] Since God gives you favor because of Christ, you can now turn your attention to serving the neighbor as your offering to God. Congregations become vocational factories, training their people for their daily lives of work and service. Work at home, school, and the office now become acts of worship. When service is our focus, all of life becomes worship. This is the true meaning behind the common term used in almost every congregation: the worship *service*.

7. Steward Your Economic Life as a Market and/or a Gift

The evangelical story recognizes that all our relationships in life have at least two economic components. This distinction is so critical that the entire life of discipleship depends on grasping its meaning. These categories, using contemporary language, are the market economy and the gift economy. The relationship between these two economies helps us understand the core message of the gospel and our relationship with God and neighbor. Confuse them and the gospel is lost.

The Market Economy

The catechism recognizes the function and flow of a normal market economy that is built on just wages and services, on production and consumption. The main insight here is that God uses these human dynamics in a sacramental manner—that is, God uses normal "business" to love and serve people. In return, people receive just and fair payment for these services. A trustworthy world is thus established. Justice reigns. God's love flows through us to the world. Luther's goal was to transform the market economy, using our language today, from a rational system driven by self-interest, into one driven by service and love of neighbor.[9]

The Gift Economy

The catechism describes here what economists today refer to as a "gift economy." A gift economy is a mode of exchange where valuables are not traded or sold but given without any explicit agreement for immediate or future rewards.[10]

The overarching message of the Apostles' Creed is that God's activities in the world reflect a gift economy. All is a gift. God is in the business of giving gifts to God's people—creation, redemption, and holiness through the Spirit. These are gifts that cannot be earned or deserved. Our response to these gifts should be praise, gratitude, and obedience.

Freedom sets the tone. This kind of economy is meant to build relationships and communities. It's a basic form of social interaction. God gives gifts freely. In response, God's gifts liberate us to give gifts to God like praise, prayer, and service.

All our relationships are based on both economies. Even in our families, we experience both market and gift economies. Justice and grace. Law and gospel. For Luther, the catechism teaches how our relationships with God and neighbor rely on both economies and which economy is used at which time and for what purpose.

8. Speak Daily Blessings and Thanksgivings (Lord, Teach Us to Bless . . .)

Learn how to sanctify life by prayer. This is a wonderful dimension of the catechism where Luther teaches how to bless life. The day starts with a blessing, a morning prayer, and ends with a word of thanksgiving. Each meal also includes blessings and thanksgivings. This dual prayer over food will strike many as a strange practice. However, it is an ancient one. It sets the tone for daily prayer. At the beginning of the day: "Lord, bless my work today." At the end of work: "Lord, thank you for a good and productive day." At the beginning of a meeting: "Lord, bless our time of work together." At the end of the meeting: "Lord, thank you for your faithfulness to our collective efforts." The pattern of blessing and thanksgiving can penetrate our whole lives, if we can practice this pattern at our tables and at bedsides every day. This spiritual practice can help us "pray without ceasing," even at work (1 Thess 5:16–18).

HOW THESE INSIGHTS CHANGED MY MINISTRY

Here are five examples of how the insights described above have brought structural changes to how I approach ministry today. I hope future lessons will also be learned as I hear about the practices of other leaders and congregations.

Listen to People at Work and Home

Visit people at work. This has become a new spiritual practice. During these thirty-to-sixty-minute visits, I ask people how they connect their faith with their work. I listen. What I learn is how people understand the story of God, what role their work plays in that drama, and who mentored them in connecting faith and work in this way. These are some of the richest faith encounters I've experienced in my ministry.

So ask your pastor to visit you at work. Talk to them about how you connect your faith and your work. Be a good storyteller.

Structure the Congregation as a Vocational Center

This may be the biggest challenge for congregational ministry. How does a congregation organize its ministry around vocation?[11] Mission literature is filled with wonderful admonitions about how a congregation should organize itself to do mission.

The focus on vocational training, nevertheless, proposes an alternative missional vision. The focus on vocation is first not on the mission of the *church* but on that of the *people of God* from Monday through Saturday. Its emphasis is not on the gathered but on the scattered community. Its goal is to help train God's people not just for their church work but also for their callings at home, at their places of work, and in their communities. If our people's work is their pulpit, how do we prepare them to minister from that lofty place as worker-priests? Formation thus becomes a lifelong engagement with the eighth day of creation story.

One suggestion seems obvious: the laity must be empowered to lead. As our people constantly discern their callings at home, work, school, and church and in their neighborhoods, the congregation needs to be a place where they can turn for training as disciples and worker-priests in their daily lives. Congregations must change dramatically in their focus and structure if vocation is to become central in their missional imaginations. The first step toward this change is lay leadership being empowered to lead.

Use Faith, Work, and Economics to "Make Disciples"

As the missional focus has changed in the congregation, so too has my preaching and teaching. Faith, work, and economic issues now dominate my preaching and teaching. The key focus is to become more of a spiritual resource for laity. My visits to work sites inform the content.

Ask for Bible studies, discipleship training, sermons, and workshops that focus on faith, work, and economics. This emphasis will lead to new understandings of eighth-day discipleship.

Ask Economic Questions: God Is in the Numbers

Here's a not-so-secret secret about clergy. Pastors and priests tend to love people and hate numbers. Clergy are trained to lead communities, engage people with the gospel, and tend to the sick and dying. With these skill sets, budgets tend to confuse or irritate them. So also do charts, graphs, cash-flow statements, and foundation investments. However, congregational leaders and pastors today must embrace numbers as one of the keys to proclaiming the gospel. The numbers are not just about accountability; they are about discerning God's movement and our mission. Lay leaders get this. They understand the importance of finances and other tangible assessments in telling a story about God's activities in a congregation, business, family, and community.

Don't let clergy overlook important numbers. On the flip side, clergy should help their lay leaders read numbers theologically and choose which numbers might best reflect the theology of the congregation. Incarnation, in all its forms, values numbers.

Turn the Church's Focus Inside Out

If your congregation didn't exist, what difference would that make for your community? A church that commits to vocation and God's economic story in Christ will necessarily find itself living deeply within the neighborhood. The church isn't a club. It's a ministry that must point itself outward. A congregation's membership should always be trained to focus on their ministries in daily life. The issues encountered by making this shift will be difficult and complex, including those related to the church's budget. Lay leaders will be invaluable as guides to and interpreters of their various vocational worlds, since many clergy don't get the language and culture of the business community. I can assure you that once a church takes the step to turn outward toward the community, the life of the church changes. The church goes where it sees God at work. Mission becomes fascinating—and unpredictable.

LIVING WITHIN THE EIGHTH DAY OF CREATION STORY

The creation of the world, as told by Genesis, includes a God who creates, separates, and names.[12] What is amazing about this creation story is that God invites Adam, God's very creation, to participate in God's own job as the chief gardener. It's a stunning invitation. Creation and vocation happened simultaneously! Adam is invited to join God and cocreate the garden—that is, creating, separating, filling, governing, producing, naming, and being fruitful. God adds humanity as a business partner! A genuine collaborator. The lesson here is a powerful one, although somewhat surprising. Our invitation is to work in the places where God is already gardening. Our reality is constantly being created and re-created by God through our work *with* God. All economic plans start with this insightful story about creation. God is the chief steward, the manager-in-chief, the good Gardner: "So out of the ground the Lord God formed every animal of the field and every bird of the air, and brought them to the man to see what he would call them; and whatever the man called every living creature, that was its name. The man gave names to all cattle, and to the birds of the air, and to every animal of the field" (Gen 2:19–20).

God shares the work with Adam. In essence, God's command is to complete creation by naming things, as well as "to till and keep" the garden (Gen 2:15). Preservation, care, and service are what is meant by "to till and to keep." Ruling is implied by "naming." Dominion and guardianship are both vocational calls at creation. Our initial job description therefore involves a balancing act of multiple callings. Gardens need constant care and cultivation. They also need order and structure.

The overarching message here is that Adam's call to "have dominion" (Gen 1:28) and "to till and keep" the garden (Gen 2:15) are fundamentally economic vocations. The same is true in Genesis 1 when Adam and Eve are to "be fruitful and multiply, and fill the earth" (Gen 1:28). Some refer to this text as the "cultural mandate." This mandate involves planning, working, tilling, caring, harvesting, guarding, naming, and conceptualizing the world with the goal of human thriving. Furthermore, these economic vocations have remained in force, even after the fall. Noah, as proof, receives this same call from God.

Yet surprisingly, the whole biblical story confirms that we can't reenter the garden. After the fall, the gate is closed and locked. An angel still stands at the east entrance to the garden with a flaming sword. But our mandate to work doesn't change, as Noah discovered, though the environment, conditions, and context in which the mandate must be fulfilled are now radically different. We lost access to Eden because of our sin and rebellion; therefore, we are no longer able to walk with God in the cool of the day, and we now know good and evil like God, but apart from God. Grappling with those changes while still hearing the call to work is one of the chief responsibilities of any Christian disciple.

It's fascinating that the New Testament proclamation of Jesus largely leaves the garden of Eden behind and, therefore, any ideology about the "order of creation" rooted in that idyllic state. We often desire to go back and experience Eden. We are curious. We want to know what it was like to live with God, walking and working in Eden.

But we can't. Jesus calls us to live in a new city, a city where he is the temple, the river of life, the door, and the tree of life. All the old metaphors are transformed because Jesus calls us into the future and into the new city of God. After the resurrection, God's big plan is not merely to restore but to redeem and re-create. Building a new city is the goal, not merely a renovation plan for the old garden. Our call is twofold: to care for and preserve the first creation and to simultaneously work with the Holy Spirit on "a new heaven and earth." Amazingly, this vision includes a new heaven! It is Jesus who is central to this home economics project. This is eighth-day spirituality. As such, it demands a new architecture:

> "Come, I will show you the bride, the wife of the Lamb." And in the spirit he carried me away to a great, high mountain and showed me the holy city Jerusalem coming down out of heaven from God. It has the glory of God and a radiance like a very rare jewel, like jasper, clear as crystal. It has a great, high wall with twelve gates, and at the gates twelve angels, and on the gates are inscribed the names of the twelve tribes of the Israelites. . . . I saw no temple in the city, for its temple is the Lord God the Almighty and the Lamb. And the city has no need of sun or moon to shine on it, for the glory of God is its light, and its lamp is the Lamb. . . . Its gates will never be shut by day—and there will be no night there. (Rev 21:9–12, 22–23, 25)

As we enter more deeply into the biblical story using faith, work, and economics as architectural guides, we find ourselves living between two economic stories, those of the garden of Eden and of New Jerusalem. The garden in our past and the New Jerusalem in our future. Both "places" call and influence us daily. We are still intrigued by how God created the world. Naturally, sin has greatly affected how we experience creation. We are never quite sure whether we're seeing the new creation or whether it's our sinful flesh calling us from the old. It's complicated. We know that cherubim guard the east door of the garden. We're blocked from fully tasting fruit from the tree of life until Jesus returns. Even though we now have the power to know good and evil, that power is fuzzy and so often disappoints because it functions without God. It serves us at some moments; it mocks us at others. Our desire is just to walk again with God in the cool of the day.

We also pray daily for the kingdom of God "to come": "Come, Lord Jesus." The Bible describes the city coming down like a bride, using amazing architectural language. The picture of the holy city coming down from heaven is fantastic! Notice: Not only do we await life within the walls of New Jerusalem, but we are the city itself. This is what awaits us, streets of gold and pearly gates. But wait, there's more! John's Gospel affirms that "eternal life," life in the city of God, starts now when we believe in the Son of God. Paul also affirms, "So if anyone is in Christ, there is a new creation!" (2 Cor 5:17). Through faith, we experience a relationship with God through Christ that provides various foretastes of the coming kingdom. We'd like to taste more of the banquet now, to be honest. Nevertheless, even as a series of spiritual appetizers, the banquet has begun. The church is a sign, instrument, and foretaste of the coming kingdom. That is hard to believe, sometimes. Gems don't line the walls of our aging congregations. The front doors of our parishes act nothing like pearly gates of hospitality. Congregational fellowship can seem dark, at times, without the light of Christ. Nevertheless, by faith, we affirm that the church as an eighth-day holy city is a major gift we've been given. Although we can taste a little heaven now, death is a hurdle until we can experience an economy that can afford streets of gold and beautiful mansions, where want is eliminated, and all our tears are wiped away. That's Christ's economy in New Jerusalem.

The mission of the Triune God is to start building a new heaven and earth today. That work started with the death, resurrection, and ascension of Jesus. Jesus sits on the throne of God and reigns. He tells us, in effect, "Go therefore . . . and work for the new city." Start building! In some ways, this is an exciting mandate. Working with God again, constructing the walls of the New Jerusalem, now through the Holy Spirit. It's so exciting that we might be tempted with a certain brand of triumphalism. On the other hand, it's frustrating because we see God's purposes so dimly; we struggle to see what is the new and what is the old creation. Are we preserving the old in our congregation or creating something new? Where is God at work here? This is a humble task. There's no room for triumphalism here.

But this is the call and our mission. This is the chief job of all preaching, teaching, and evangelism. Go therefore . . . God is building a new city . . . till and keep it. It's this message that connects Sunday and Monday for all worker-priests. We are called to live in two stories simultaneously, in the first creation and the new creation: the first creation, marred by sin, and the new creation that breaks into life sporadically and gives us joy. Here we stand. It's a position of humility. It's a position of anticipation. God will finally build the city. Not us. God's work, yes, but our hands. That fact alone produces hope.

The great Sunday-Monday divorce was part of my religious inheritance. This is why I was so fascinated with the eight-sided churches in Greece and Turkey. The eighth-day experience of the resurrection was so important to these early Christians that they designed an octagonal building to remind them of their mission and their Lord's activity at the right hand of the Father. An eight-sided church lifts the eyes to the new creation. Eighth-day churches desire to preserve the old, yes, but they also desire to create something new through creativity and innovation, death and resurrection. The entrepreneurial spirit truly lies within the freedom and responsibility of Christians working for the eighth day of creation.

Our goal is to preach the resurrection on Sunday to empower the people of God to live in the eternal eighth day of creation. Eighth-day churches move forward with the project of the new creation. Freedom and responsibility reign in this movement forward. Breaking norms with their freedom and responsibility for these Christians is their birthright.

The gospel remains the hope of the world. What I've learned since 2012 is that the tones and hues of the eighth day of creation story can be rediscovered and admired afresh when the topics of faith, work, and economics are used to explore the biblical narrative. Each brings out the beauty of the other, like the facets of a diamond. Together, they uncover dimensions of the gospel that my tradition has long overlooked or mostly forgotten.

Through the catechism, I've learned about the architecture of eight-sided buildings. It's within this edifice that I now desire to live, worship, and serve as an eighth-day disciple.

Study Guide

This book is designed for communal and congregational discussion and discernment. The following questions are offered to assist with this dialogue and to encourage imagination around these topics.

Introduction: An Evangelical Architecture for Eighth-Day Discipleship

1. Have you ever seen an eight-sided church? How does the opening story about the author's encounter with an eight-sided church stir your imagination?
2. Have you ever heard of the eighth day of creation? How does this concept stir your imagination about discipleship?
3. The author talks about three key design elements for building a life of discipleship. What are these three keys? In what ways do these keys surprise you or raise questions?

Chapter 1: Building Discipleship to Withstand Economic Storms

1. *Houston, we have a problem!* How have you experienced economic issues in your life? Like a roller coaster? A storm? A virus? How have you been taught to adapt?
2. In what ways are the following problematic?
   - the separation of faith and economics
   - the separation of Sunday and Monday
   - the separation of the sacred and the secular
3. Individuals and congregations are impacted by economic realities and challenges. How often do you think about or discuss such realities in the context of matters of faith and discipleship?

4. What portion or percentage of your daily life is involved with work and/or economic issues?

5. Have you ever been out of work? What effect did your joblessness have on your spiritual life? Have you ever been in debt? What effect did your indebtedness have on your spirituality?

6. The chapter reviews four worldviews that compete with the gospel for your attention:
   a. moralistic therapeutic deism
   b. *homo economicus*
   c. the prosperity gospel
   d. tribalism
   Where or how have you noticed one or all these world-views in your family, in school, at work, in the marketplace, or at church?

7. Using architecture as a metaphor, which architectural build-ing from your city or town best describes your spiritual life? Are there areas in your city or town that have been "architec-turally" isolated from vital economic activity?

8. How might you use the ideas of faith, work, and economics to approach different dimensions of your Christian life?

Chapter 2: Connecting Faith and Work

1. How do you connect your faith and your work?

2. Do you believe that God is loving the world through you at work? At home? In your neighborhood? Can you give an example?

3. Did someone teach you how to make this connection between faith and work (e.g., a parent, mentor, coworker, or pastor), or did you learn how on your own?

4. What resources have you used to connect faith and work? Scripture? Books? Articles? Movies? Seminars? Podcasts? Web-sites? The catechism? Something else?

5. David Miller, in his book, *God at Work*, maps out four ways to connect faith and work, which are summarized below. Which of these approaches most closely describes your life? You can choose more than one.

    a. Ethics: I do work based on an ethical code I learned at church.

    b. Evangelism: I share my faith at work either directly or indirectly.

    c. Experience: I do my work because I feel called by God to do it.

    d. Enrichment: I feel fulfilled because I'm using the gifts with which God has blessed me.

6. Have you ever seen an eight-sided church? An eight-sided baptismal font? Did you know the meaning behind the use of the eight sides?

7. How did this chapter describe the difference between the Sabbath and the Lord's Day? Which term do you use in your own observance of the Sabbath commandment? Why?

8. Will there be work in heaven? Explain.

Chapter 3: Eighth-Day Christians:
Living in God's Home Economics Project

1. What is your experience with home economics? Positive or negative?

2. How does home economics help you imagine God's management of the world? How about the biblical image of "tilling and keeping the garden" in Genesis 2?

3. The definition of *economics* involves so many activities: management, stewardship, planning, governance, dispensations, financial budgets, and more. Which of these activities do you associate most closely with economics? Which ones were a surprise?

4. In Matthew 28, the call to mission for the disciples is set in the context of the story of Jesus's ascension to the throne of God. What connection does this story have to economics?

5. What is "God's economy"? Describe it. How do you see God's economy functioning in the world? Where does it not seem to be functioning?

6. How does the Bible use the word *economics*, as laid out in this chapter?

7. Economic numbers tell a story. What story might your checkbook tell? What is the story behind your church's budget? What stories describe the underserved areas of your city? The US economy has a big story. How would you summarize that story?

8. "God is in the numbers." Explain what this might mean for you, your family, your neighborhood, your community, and your congregation.

Chapter 4: The Catechism and the Ten Commandments: Law as the First Key to an Evangelical Design

1. The basic three pillars of teaching discipleship are the Ten Commandments, the Apostles' Creed, and the Lord's Prayer. Where did you first learn these three pillars? In Sunday school? In confirmation classes? As an adult? Or did these pillars not play an important role in your faith formation?

2. When you reflect on the Ten Commandments, how do you think of them? How many of these statements do you agree with?
   a. I take the Ten Commandments literally.
   b. I see the Ten Commandments as summarizing natural law.
   c. I see the Ten Commandments as a general call to justice.
   d. I see the Ten Commandments as a way to apply biblical principles to my life and to society.
   e. The Ten Commandments are a tool that helps me discover my need for Christ.
   f. Other.

3. What does it mean that God's law functions like leaves and leather? How does the story of God clothing Adam and Eve help explain how God's law functions in your life?

4. How does God's law function like a curb, rule, mirror, and X-ray machine? Can you imagine another metaphor that might also work to describe God's law?

5. Each of the commandments includes a teaching on faith, work, and economics. What do these teachings mean for your life personally? Or your congregation? Or your neighborhood?

6. Why is the First Commandment understood as the most important? Why is it often said that all the commandments flow from the First Commandment?

7. Luther explains the Fourth Commandment ("Honor your father and your mother") as the "vocational commandment." How does Luther move from the command to honor parents to honoring all those with authority to serve us in our lives?

8. How does reflecting on the Ten Commandments help connect Sunday with Monday?

Chapter 5: The Catechism and Creed:
Redemption as the Second Key to an Evangelical Design

1. How does the *Small Catechism* connect the first article of the Apostles' Creed (i.e., on creation) to economic activities? Is the message that "all is a gift" good news or bad news?

2. Luther's explanation of the first article of the creed reviews the gifts that he had received from God. How does the first article help you see God as generous? What list of gifts would you make?

3. The second article of the Apostles' Creed ties two ideas together: "Jesus is Lord" and "redemption." How does the *Small Catechism* explain this connection?

4. How might you answer the two questions posed by D. James Kennedy concerning the assurance of eternal life and heaven?

How do these questions clarify the second article of the Apostles' Creed?

5. Why does the second article use an economic term (i.e., redemption) to explain our salvation through Christ?

6. The New Testament talks about Jesus's Lordship and reign in terms of a new economy. Do you envision Jesus on the throne of God managing and stewarding the world through you and your work? Why or why not?

7. The third article of the Apostles' Creed makes it clear that life in the kingdom is tied to faith, freedom, and service. This is the work of the Holy Spirit. How does the Spirit's work of the kingdom connect Sunday and Monday in your own experience?

8. What role does the Spirit play in your work? In your economic life?

Chapter 6: The Catechism and the Lord's Prayer:
The Kingdom of God as the Third Key to an Evangelical Design

1. How often do you use the Lord's Prayer during the week? Why is this?

2. Have you ever prayed the Lord's Prayer at a public event, like a football game? Describe the event. Why was the Lord's Prayer used?

3. Explain these two affirmations:
    a. Commandments lead to the need for redemption.
    b. Redemption leads to prayer for the kingdom.

4. The Lord's Prayer makes a fascinating connection between "sin" and "debt." Why did Jesus make this connection between economic and noneconomic issues?

5. Why does the *Small Catechism* make a connection between the petition for "daily bread" in the Lord's Prayer and the first article of the Apostles' Creed?

6. How do you understand "daily bread"? What is the connection between this daily bread and the kingdom of God?

7. Why might Luther want us to include the Apostles' Creed and the Lord's Prayer in our daily prayers at home?
8. Why do some church liturgical traditions pray the Lord's Prayer right before receiving communion?

Chapter 7: Building Eighth-Day Disciples:
Five More Foundational Keys for Mission and Ministry

1. Why does the ordering of the catechism matter to our life on Monday?
2. How does an understanding of all eight parts of the catechism assist you in your walk of discipleship? Do you think you need all eight parts? Why or why not?
3. Baptism is a onetime experience, so why are we taught in the catechism to experience it daily? Are you a "daily baptist"? If not, what benefit do you see in being one?
4. Describe how the whole communion experience functions as a sign, instrument, and foretaste of an eight-sided drama of the new creation.
5. In response to the word of God, we offer gifts of gratitude: prayers and praise, bread, wine, and money. How do these symbols of gratitude—the offering—reflect our daily lives on Monday? How are they signs of your gratitude?
6. Why was the rite of confession and absolution called the Office of the Keys? Asking for forgiveness seems to act like a key to a door. How is this true in your experience?
7. The spiritual practice of saying a blessing before a meal and a word of thanksgiving after the meal is an ancient one, practiced by Jesus himself. How were you taught to pray at the table? If practiced in your daily life, how might speaking "blessings" and "thanksgivings" every day reflect an eight-sided discipleship?
8. The Table of Duties lists Bible passages that can help us define and live out our various vocations. How might such lists be used to focus us on God's call? How might such a list help or hurt us in practicing eighth-day obedience?

Chapter 8: Eighth-Day Discipleship in an Eight-Sided Church: Living by
Faith with Responsibility and Freedom

1. The gospel narrative witnessed through Scripture is challenged
    by many counternarratives or worldviews in our culture. Four
    are reintroduced and described in this chapter:
    a. moralistic therapeutic deism
    b. *homo economicus*
    c. the prosperity gospel
    d. tribalism
    Now that you have a deeper understanding of econom-
    ics, faith, and work, how have these been a force in your life?
    Describe their influence.
2. How might Luther's catechism help you challenge these
    counter-worldviews in your life?
3. What might it mean for you to live within an evangelical
    architecture that includes all eight pillars of the catechism: the
    Ten Commandments, the Apostles' Creed, the Lord's Prayer,
    baptism, communion, confession (the Office of the Keys),
    blessings, and the Table of Duties?
4. Using Luther's use of "masks of God," how is God serving the
    neighbor through you?
5. Do you experience worship as a service to God and/or
    neighbor (e.g., worship service)? Do you experience work as
    worship?
6. In what ways do numbers tell stories in your personal life
    (e.g., those in your checkbook, bank statements, ATM
    receipts, etc.)? In what ways do your congregational numbers
    tell a story?
7. If you were to paint a picture of God's activities in the world,
    what would it look like? If your congregation were to paint a
    similar picture, would it differ from yours?
8. How might you implement the following evangelical practices
    as an eighth-day Christian?
    a. Become a storyteller of the gospel.
    b. Practice daily baptism.

c. Practice Sabbath rest and work.
d. Pray the catechism.
e. Learn to wield the Lord's Prayer.
f. Practice work as worship.
g. Steward your economic relationships.
h. Speak daily blessings and thanksgivings.

Notes

Foreword

1 LW 31:25. Throughout, citations to this work come from *Luther's Works*, American ed. (Philadelphia: Fortress, 1955–86).
2 LW 36:39.

Introduction

1 "Category: Octagonal Churches," Wikipedia, last modified October 23, 2015, 20:58, https://en.wikipedia.org/wiki/Category:Octagonal_churches.
2 I am thankful to Evangelical Lutheran Church in America bishop Wayne Miller for this marvelous phrase.

Chapter 1: Building Discipleship to Withstand Economic Storms

1 In the 1995 docudrama *Apollo 13*, the famous line appears as follows: "Uh, Houston, we had a problem."
2 See Liz Hampton and Ernest Scheyder, "Houston Still Rebuilding from 2017 Floods as New Hurricane Season Arrives," Reuters, June 1, 2018, https://www.reuters.com/article/us-usa-weather-houston-housing-feature/houston-still-rebuilding-from-2017-floods-as-new-hurricane-season-arrives-idUSKCN1IX48C.
3 See Hampton and Scheyder.
4 Richard Nelson Bolles, *What Color Is Your Parachute?* (Berkeley, CA: Ten Speed Press, 1970).
5 See Jennifer Senior, "More People Will Be Fired in the Pandemic. Let's Talk about It," *New York Times*, June 22, 2020, https://nytimes.com/2020/06/14/opinion/layoffs-coronavirus-economy.amp.html.
6 Christian Smith with Melinda Lundquist Denton, *Soul Searching: The Religious and Spiritual Lives of American Teenagers* (New York: Oxford University Press, 2009), 171. I am grateful to Pastor Jason Van Hunnik for introducing me to this resource.

7 Smith with Lundquist Denton, 176.

8 For another list of counternarratives to the gospel, see Paul Dietterich, *Foretaste: Leadership for the Missional Church* (Eugene, OR: Cascade, 2019). His includes nationalism, individualism, consumerism, racism, sexism, fear, and violence (84).

Chapter 2: Connecting Faith and Work

1 See Hugh Whelchel, *How Then Should We Work? Rediscovering the Biblical Doctrine of Work* (Bloomington, IN: WestBow, 2012), 58–75.

2 Martin Luther, *The Babylonian Captivity of the Church*, in *Selected Writings of Martin Luther*, ed. Theodore G. Tappert (Minneapolis: Fortress, 2007), 430.

3 Tomáš Sedláček, *The Economics of Good and Evil* (New York: Oxford University Press, 2011), 6.

4 Found in Mark Twain's *Autobiography*, vol. 1 (Berkeley: University of California Press, 2010), 228. This particular passage was dictated in Florence in 1904.

5 The original quote, as Tomáš Sedláček points out, is, "Life isn't one damn thing after another. It's the same damn thing again and again." Sedláček, *Economics of Good and Evil*, p. 5.

6 Sedláček, 5.

7 Sedláček, 6.

8 Quoted in Gary Moore's excellent book *Faithful Finances 101: From the Poverty of Fear and Greed to the Riches of Spiritual Investing* (West Conshohocken, PA: Templeton Foundation Press, 2005), 207.

9 Rod Dreher, *The Benedict Option* (New York: Random House, 2017), 1.

10 Quoted in Peter Feuerherd, "Pope Francis' Blunt Critique of Capitalism Praised as Needed Warning," NCR, September 6, 2018, https://www.ncronline.org/news/earthbeat/pope-francis-blunt-critique-capitalism-praised-needed-warning.

11 See Pope Francis's call, at the Assisi Summit in the fall of 2020, to focus on the present state of the global economy in Ines San Martin, "Assisi Summit to Focus on Pope's Challenge to 'Pathological' Economy," Crux, June 27, 2020, https://cruxnow.com/vatican/2020/06/assisi-summit-to-focus-on-popes-challenge-to-pathological-economy/.

12 Maggie Fitzgerald, "The CEOs of Nearly 200 Companies Just Said Shareholder Value Is No Longer Their Main Objective," CNBC, August 19, 2019, https://www.cnbc.com/2019/08/19/the-ceos-of-nearly-two-hundred-companies-say-shareholder-value-is-no-longer-their-main-objective.html.

13 Fitzgerald.

14 See Fitzgerald.

15 Gene Veith, *Working for Our Neighbor: A Lutheran Primer on Vocation, Economics, and Ordinary Life* (Grand Rapids, MI: Christian's Library Press, 2016), 6.

16 See details about the number eight as a Christian symbol in Michal Hunt, "The Early Christian Symbols of the Octagon and the Fish," Agape Bible Study, May 17, 2007, https://www.agapebiblestudy.com/documents/The%20Sign%20of%20the%20Fish.htm.

17 Quoted in Joan Huyser-Honig, "Theological Reasons for Baptistry Shapes," Calvin Institute of Christian Worship, May 12, 2006, https://worship.calvin.edu/resources/resource-library/theological-reasons-for-baptistry-shapes/.

18 Quoted in Huyser-Honig.

19 One exception to this rule is Westwood Lutheran Church in Minneapolis, Minnesota. Pastor Jason Van Hunnik has elevated "vocation" together with the lead pastor Tania Haber. For the broader experience of linking faith and work within congregations, see the Made to Flourish network, https://www.madetoflourish.org/.

20 See David Miller, *God at Work: The History of the Faith and Work Movement* (New York: Oxford University Press, 2007), 125–42.

21 Miller, 82.

22 An exception to this evaluation was my missionary experience in Africa. I worked for five years in Zaire (now the Democratic Republic of Congo). An important dimension of the whole ministry was concerned with job creation, vocational discernment, and trying to work for a thriving city (Bukavu, Zaire). I can make this evaluation now with confidence but, at that time, I didn't have the vocabulary to express what was happening within the ministry.

23 The millennium in question here refers to the thousand-year reign of Christ mentioned in Revelation 20:3. Premillennialists teach that a golden age or paradise will occur on earth for a thousand years before the final judgment of the world. Another version of this teaching is that after the second coming of Christ, he will reign for a thousand years over the earth before the final judgment and the final consummation of God's redemptive purpose. Postmillennialism refers to the teaching that Christ will return after a thousand-year period in which the kingdom of God will be extended in the world and many will come to believe. Lutherans generally follow an amillennial view, meaning Christians already live in the kingdom that Christ has come to bring. We live in the tension of the "already / not yet" as we await the full realization of Christ's reign. Amillennialists don't try to set any sort of timetable for Christ's return.

24 See Hunt, "Early Christian Symbols."

25 *The Catholic Catechism*, 2nd ed. (New York: Doubleday, 1995), 100.

Chapter 3: Eighth-Day Christians

1   There are many scholars and friends who have greatly influenced my thinking around faith and economics. Their work and their ideas have impacted this chapter and the book. They are Moore, *Faithful Finances 101*; Jon Pahl, "An Economic Reading of Luther's Catechism in Long Context," in *The Forgotten Luther: Reclaiming the Social-Economic Dimension of the Reformation*, ed. Carter Lindberg and Paul Wee (Minneapolis: Lutheran University Press, 2016); Tom Nelson, *The Economics of Neighborly Love* (Downers Grove, IL: InterVarsity Press, 2017); Sedláček, *Economics of Good and Evil*; Veith, *Working for Our Neighbor*; and Timothy Wengert, *Martin Luther's Catechisms: Forming the Faith* (Minneapolis: Fortress, 2009).

2   Many authors deal with "economics" in Greek philosophy. In this regard, I suggest reading Sedláček, "Ancient Greece," chap. 3 in *Economics of Good and Evil*, 93–128.

3   Material on home economics in this section was taken from many sources. For accessible information, see "Home Economics," Wikipedia, accessed June 2019, https://en.wikipedia.org/wiki/Home_economics. The discussion in this section is focused on management and stewardship.

4   This attitude is expressed directly in official church documents. See Jordan Ballor, *Ecumenical Babel: Confusing Economic Ideology and the Church's Social Witness* (Grand Rapids, MI: Christian's Library Press, 2010).

5   Abraham Kuyper, "Sphere Sovereignty," in *Abraham Kuyper: A Centennial Reader*, ed. James D. Bratt (Grand Rapids, MI: Eerdmans, 1998), 488.

6   Bible Study Tools, s.v. "oikonomia," accessed October 5, 2021, https://www.biblestudytools.com/lexicons/greek/nas/oikonomia.html. For further references to *oikonomia*, see "3621. Oikonomeó," Bible Hub, accessed October 5, 2021, https://biblehub.com/greek/3621.htm.

7   This phrase, "What is my salvation for?" comes from the video series "For the Life of the World," published by Acton Institute, which discusses the relationship between faith and economics. See "For the Life of the World," Acton Institute, accessed October 5, 2021, https://www.acton.org/publications.

8   See Nelson, *Economics of Neighborly Love*.

9   Phyllis Anderson has written an excellent Bible study series as a part of the 1K Project for the Criterion Institute promoting microlending as a missional activity within local churches. See Phyllis Anderson, "Roadmap for Christian Denominations to Use Finance to Reduce Gender-Based Violence," Criterion Institute, August 16, 2021, https://criterioninstitute.org/explore/resources.

10 Anderson.

11 Sallie McFague, quoted in Anderson, 11.

12 I'm particularly grateful for the book edited by Lindberg and Wee, *Forgotten Luther*, which is now published and available at Fortress Press.

13 The first social welfare ordinance, the "common purse," was passed by the Wittenberg town council with Luther's assistance in late 1520 or early 1521. See Carter Lindberg, "Luther and the Common Chest," in Lindberg and Wee, *Forgotten Luther*, 21.

14 See Lindberg, 17–29.

15 Lindberg, 19.

16 See Homer's *Odyssey*, trans. Robert Fagles (New York: Pelican Books, 1996), 272–73.

17 See Brian Fikkert and Michael Rhodes, "Homo Economicus versus Homo Imago Dei," *Journal of Markets and Morality* 20, no. 1 (Spring 2017): 101–18.

18 Sedláček, *Economics of Good and Evil*, 14.

19 To be clear, rational self-interest doesn't necessarily mean greed. Adam Smith was clear on this point in 1798, although many of his admirers in subsequent years have abandoned any attempt at mixing too much ethics into economic theory.

20 I thank Pastor Jason Van Hunnik for pointing out the importance of this book.

21 Smith with Lundquist Denton, *Soul Searching*, 162–63. See Jason Van Hunnik's excellent article describing how his congregation teaches vocation entitled "Grace and Vocation: Ministry Focus-Strategy-Practice," *Currents in Mission and Theology* 46, no. 1 (January 2019): 25–32.

22 LW 43:13–14.

Chapter 4: The Catechism and the Ten Commandments

1 Pahl, "Economic Reading," 59–60. The substance of this chapter relies heavily on Jon Pahl's insights.

2 Luther, cited in Pahl, 60.

3 Moore, *Faithful Finances 101*, 27.

4 Pahl, "Economic Reading," 59.

5 Natural law is a teaching that humanity is created by God to function within a "moral order" accompanied by certain "inalienable rights." Natural law is therefore tied to how God creates and sustains the world. Our created nature comes with a moral mode of operation and an inheritance of rights that can be understood universally through human reason and the conscience, grasped naturally through the prism of culture, reason, and experience. Law does many good things in society for Luther, but ultimately, it condemns.

6   For Luther, the law of Moses that regulated work and economics for Israel at Sinai is now dead, since Christ abolished the law (Gal 3). More precisely, if you as a Christian decide to follow any of Moses's laws, you need to follow all of them. It's all or nothing. The Ten Commandments become for Luther, therefore, a summary of natural law.

7   Luther used three categories, which he borrowed from Aristotle. They were *oikonomia* (home management, which included family and business), *politia* (civil engagement), and *ecclesia* (church).

8   Many historians note that Luther wrote his catechism while his young son ran around the house asking many such questions, like "What is that?"—or, in German, "Was ist das?"

9   Throughout the following sections, I quote from Martin Luther, *Luther's "Small Catechism,"* ed. Timothy J. Wengert (Minneapolis: Fortress, 2016). This translation can be found in Augsburg Fortress' online *Small Catechism,* also available as an app.

10 Economist Robert Nelson, quoted in Sedláček, *Economics of Good and Evil,* 234.

11 Economist Robert Samuelson, quoted in Sedláček, 235.

12 Pahl, "Economic Reading," 60–61.

13 Martin Luther, "The Ten Commandments," in *The Book of Concord: The Confessions of the Evangelical Lutheran Church,* ed. Robert Kolb and Timothy J. Wengert (Minneapolis: Fortress, 2000), 387.

14 Luther, 393.

15 Pahl, "Economic Reading," 61.

16 Justo Gonzalez, *Faith and Wealth: A History of Early Christian Ideas on the Origin, Significance, and Use of Money* (San Francisco: Harper & Row, 1990), 20–21.

17 Veith, *Working for Our Neighbor,* 18. More specifically, "Luther gave as examples of the soldiers' authorization, under a Roman's 13 chain of command, to 'bear the sword' and the judges' authorization to punish criminals, while the Christian without these callings must forgive his enemies and wrongdoers." Martin Luther, "Whether Soldiers, Too, Can Be Saved," in LW 46:93–137.

18 Veith, *Working for Our Neighbor,* 3.

19 Martin Luther, "Fifth Commandment," in Kolb and Wengert, *Book of Concord,* 411.

20 Luther, 412.

21 Moore, *Faithful Finances 101,* 77.

22 Martin Luther, "Seventh Commandment," in Kolb and Wengert, *Book of Concord,* 417.

23 Wengert, *Martin Luther's Catechisms,* 36.

24 Luther, "Seventh Commandment," 419.

25 Luther, 417.

Chapter 5: The Catechism and Creed

1   Throughout the following sections, I quote from Luther, *Luther's "Small Catechism."*
2   Veith, *Working for Our Neighbor*, 17.
3   Martin Luther, "Apostles' Creed," in Kolb and Wengert, *Book of Concord*, 433.
4   Wengert, *Martin Luther's Catechisms*, 47.
5   Wengert, 47–48.
6   Quoted in Wengert, 57.
7   Quoted in Wengert, 57.
8   Wengert, 57.
9   Wengert, 55.
10 Anselm's theory proposed that God purchased us from the devil through Christ's death as a ransom. Although this theory is still taught as "orthodoxy" in some churches, this teaching is fraught with problems both theological and spiritual.
11 D. James Kennedy, *Evangelism Explosion*, 3rd ed. (Wheaton, IL: Tyndale, 1983).
12 Kennedy, 16.
13 Wengert, *Martin Luther's Catechisms*, 6.
14 Quoted in Wengert, 7.
15 Veith, *Working for Our Neighbor*, 2.

Chapter 6: The Catechism and the Lord's Prayer

1   From Martin Luther, *Luther's Prayers*, ed. Herbert F. Brokering (Minneapolis: Augsburg Fortress, 1994), 50:

> To this day I suckle at the Lord's Prayer like a child, and as an old man eat and drink from it and never get my fill. It is the very best prayer, even better than the psalter, which is so very dear to me. It is surely evident that a real master composed and taught it. What a great pity that the prayer of such a master is prattled and chattered so irreverently all over the world! How many pray the Lord's Prayer several thousand times in the course of a year, and if they were to keep on doing so for a thousand years they would not have tasted nor prayer one iota, one dot, of it! In a word, the Lord's Prayer is the greatest martyr on earth (as are the name and Word of God). Everybody tortures and abuses it; few take comfort and joy in its proper use.

2   For a present-day example of sin and debt forgiveness being linked, see Elizabeth Bruenig, "Churches Step in Where Politicians Will Not," opinion, *New York Times*, November 27, 2020.

3   Throughout the following sections, I quote from Luther, *Luther's "Small Catechism."*

4   Quoted in Brant Pietre, "The Lord's Prayer and the New Exodus," *Letter and Spirit* 2 (2006): 69–96.

5   Veith, *Working for Our Neighbor*, 2.

6   Wengert, *Martin Luther's Catechisms*, 151–52.

7   Pahl, "Economic Reading," 55.

8   Lindberg, "Luther and the Common Chest," 18.

9   Robert Kolb, "To Milk Cows and Govern Kingdoms," *Concordia Journal* 39, no. 2 (Spring 2011): 135.

10 Veith, *Working for Our Neighbor*, 1.

Chapter 7: Building Eighth-Day Disciples

1   Throughout the following sections, I quote from Luther, *Luther's "Small Catechism."*

2   "But as for one who is ignorant of the fundamentals—namely 'the power of sin,' 'the law' and 'grace'—I do not see how I can call him a Christian. For from these things Christ is known, since *to know Christ means to know his benefits* and not, as they [the scholastics] teach, to reflect upon his natures and the modes of his incarnation. For unless you know why Christ put on flesh and was nailed to the cross, what good will it do you to know merely the history about him?" Philip Melanchthon, *Loci communes*, quoted in Ignatius W. C. Van Wyk, "Philipp Melanchthon: An Introduction," *HTS Teologiese Studies* 73, no. 1 (August 29, 2017): nn18–19, https://hts.org.za/index.php/hts/article/view/4672.

3   This section from Luther's *Small Catechism* has been edited for language and length to construct a Table of Duties that communicates for audiences today what Luther was trying to accomplish in his day. For Luther's original text with helpful notes, see Martin Luther, "The Household Chart of Some Bible Passages," in Kolb and Wengert, *Book of Concord*, 365–67.

Chapter 8: Eighth-Day Discipleship in an Eight-Sided Church

1   For a bold statement about the power of story in faith communities, see Matthew Gorkos, *The Storied Church: A Strategy for Congregational Renewal* (Minneapolis: Fortress, 2021).

2   Lindberg, "Luther and the Common Chest," 19–20. Carter Lindberg quotes Luther heavily in this section. Please see the original article for references.

3   Gerhard Forde, *Where God Meets Man: Luther's Down to Earth Approach to the Gospel* (Minneapolis: Augsburg, 1972), 58.

4   All the details surrounding Wanamaker's life and work are taken from Nicole C. Kirk's excellent book, *Wanamaker's Temple: The Business of Religion in an Iconic Department Store* (New York: NYU Press, 2018).

5   Kirk, 23, 196.

6   Kirk, 193.

7   Kirk, 194–95.

8   In Hebrew, the word *avodah* is the root word for "worship," "service," and "work."

9   Adam Smith's "invisible hand" in the economy might be understood as the function of natural law in the commandments; the goal is to move beyond this invisible hand of providence toward service and love.

10 See Alex Gendler, "What Is a Gift Economy?," TED-Ed, accessed October 28, 2021, https://www.ted.com/talks/alex_gendler_what_is_a_gift_economy/transcript?language=en.

11 I've learned a lot from Pastor Jason Van Hunnik at Westwood Lutheran Church in Minneapolis, Minnesota. He has worked in this congregation for years to center their church life around the teaching of vocation.

12 Sedláček, *Economics of Good and Evil*, 58.